GURDJIEFF UNVEILED

GURDJIEFF UNVEILED:

AN OVERVIEW AND INTRODUCTION TO GURDJIEFF'S TEACHING

For the begining student, for the inquiring seeker,
and for the simply curious

Seymour B. Ginsburg

Lighthouse Workbooks

Gurdjieff related books www.lighthouse-editions.com

First published 2005
Lighthouse Workbooks
an imprint of Lighthouse Editions Limited
Gurdjieff related books www.lighthouse-editions.com

British Library Cataloguing-in-Publication Data
A catalogue record for this book is available from the British Library

ISBN 1-904998-01-1

Dedicated to

Nicolas Tereshchenko

A serious seeker, a true scholar, a friend

Sy Ginsburg and Nicolas Tereshchenko, Portland, Maine, March 2000.

Acknowledgements

An earlier book, *Gurdjieff: A New Introduction to His Teaching* (privately published, 1994) served for almost 10 years as the text for an introductory course on Gurdjieff's teaching. Supplies had run out, but a student, Rosemary Hutchinson, who liked the book very much, asked that it be reprinted again for new students. Although I knew from experience with the earlier book that a major revision was needed, it was her urging that finally caused me to undertake this new volume for which she made numerous suggestions. Other long-time students of Gurdjieff's teaching, John Amaral, Dr Keith Buzzell, William Murphey, and Professor Paul Beekman Taylor, were all kind enough to read early drafts. Each of them constructively criticized the text, making many useful recommendations. Another student, my wife Dorothy Usiskin, not only commented on the text but encouraged my effort when encouragement was needed. Many of the comments, suggestions, and recommendations of these fellow students have found their way into the text and have undoubtedly improved it. However, their help in no way constitutes an endorsement of the text by any of them. In fact, one or more of them disagreed with many of the statements that appear. Assertions with which a reader may disagree fall entirely on my shoulders. Much of the text and many of the assertions in it reflect the views of my mentor of 19 years, Sri Madhava Ashish (née Alexander Phipps, 1920–1997), who is quoted extensively.

Lighthouse Editions Limited wishes to thank the publisher, New Paradigm Books (http://www.newpara.com), for permission to reprint associated passages from *In Search of the Unitive Vision: Letters of Sri Madhava Ashish to an American Businessman, 1978–1997*, compiled with a commentary by Seymour B. Ginsburg. *Quest* magazine (formerly *The American Theosophist*) has kindly given permission to quote passages from that journal and Triangle Books has likewise given permission to quote from Gurdjieff's books *Beelzebub's Tales to His Grandson* and *Views From the Real World*.

CONTENTS

List of Tables

List of Diagrams

Foreword

Ever since the establishment of his Institute for the Harmonious Development of Man near Fontainbleau in 1922, the ideas of the Armenian sage George Ivanovich Gurdjieff (1866?–1949) have continued to attract a dedicated and often distinguished train of followers. Each in their own fashion, his principal pupils, P.D. Ouspensky, A.R. Orage, J.G. Bennett, Maurice Nicoll, and Rodney Collin sought to organize and develop Gurdjieff's system, thereby proving its resilience and vigour as a body of esoteric teachings into the twenty-first century.

The Work, the name by which his teachings are most usually known, is drawn from alchemy, where the Great Work signified the refinement and purification of base metals into gold as well as the transmutation of the soul into a higher spiritual state. Gurdjieff's teachings similarly aimed at the transformation of man's inner substance. Through cosmological speculations, through lectures, manual work, communal life, and sacred dances or 'Movements' in successive phases of his life, Gurdjieff offered a practical form of esoteric instruction that could harmonize the microcosm of the human being with the macrocosm of the universe and so reunite man with the Endlessness or supreme deity.

Much has and can be written about Gurdjieff's teachings. Pupils who knew Gurdjieff personally typically emphasized his power and charisma, while other followers of the Work have typically emphasized the uniqueness of his esoteric instruction as it impinged on their own lives. However, these personal and experiential estimates of Gurdjieff's importance have frequently overlooked his status as a major participant within a Western esoteric tradition reaching back through the modern occult revival to the Renaissance and thence to Hellenistic antiquity.

As Seymour Ginsburg relates in his preface, his introduction to Gurdjieff coincided with an understanding of esotericism as a form of teaching intended to expand human consciousness for the purposes of discovering who we are, what is our purpose, and what is the nature of reality. As in the famous words of the Emerald Tablet of Hermes Trismegistus "As above, so below", esoteric philosophy always seeks to link the microcosm with the macrocosm through a system of correspondences, hierarchies, and intermediaries. The resultant interaction of cosmology and anthropology leads to a meaningful location of man in the universe and the transmutation of the human soul through the understanding of identity, significance and purpose.

This book is a remarkable distillation of Gurdjieff's teachings within that wider awareness of Western esotericism. Following Gurdjieff's own techniques, the book is first and foremost a practical guide, beginning with the fundamental proposition that humans must be awakened to self-awareness, to the realisation that behind our "personality", influenced by any number of circumstances, lies our "essence", which is our identity with the universal. The teaching is thus not about attainment of something that is missing, so much as the discovery or awareness of our real identity. Alongside Gurdjieff''s teachings relating to the transmutation of energy within the context of his complex cosmology, Ginsburg provides stepped lessons in the raising of one's consciousness, with techniques for increasing attentiveness and the conservation of our intellectual and spiritual energies. Other chapters address the practice of meditation and recommendations for organizing a Gurdjieff group, involving music, sacred dance, and readings from *Beelzebub's Tales to His Grandson*.

While the principal thrust of this guide is practical esotericism, an interesting appendix throws important light on Gurdjieff's own debt to Western esotericism. The sources of his teachings long remained obscure, supposedly drawn from the mingled influences of Eastern Christianity and Sufism in the multicultural patchwork of the Caucasus and Central Asia. However, Ginsburg also traces Gurdjieff's inspiration to the modern occult revival, in particular to the work of Helena Petrovna Blavatsky (1831–1891), the founder of modern Theosophy. Blavatsky's major work *The Secret Doctrine* (1888) comprised two volumes devoted respectively to cosmogenesis and anthropogenesis. She claimed that the work was at least partly inspired by her two teachers or mahatmas, masters of wisdom resident at a secret centre in Tibet. Blavatsky promised more practical teaching in a later volume and also hinted at the advent of another teacher to be sent by the masters of wisdom. As Ginsburg shows, Gurdjieff had high-level contacts in the Theosophical Society, including two editors involved in the publication of the Mahatma Letters. Ginsburg's suggestions of Gurdjieff's debt to Theosophy are amply confirmed by the recent research of Sophia Wellbeloved into the numerological parallels between their cosmologies.

Thanks to the pioneering work of Professor Antoine Faivre at the Sorbonne, the Western esoteric spirituality is at last finding recognition as a coherent subject of academic study. Whether or not Gurdjieff's teaching can be regarded as the fulfilment of Blavatsky's prophecy, his system for the transformation of consciousness represents a major example of applied Western esotericism. Ginsburg's concise and masterly study serves as an ideal introductory guide to its practice and provenance. It will be of interest both to practitioners and students who wish to understand Gurdjieff in a wider context.

Dr Nicholas Goodrick-Clarke
Director, Centre for Western Esotericism
University of Wales Lampeter

Preface

Gurdjieff Unveiled is a new overview of and introduction to the teaching of G.I. Gurdjieff. In 1994, an earlier book entitled *Gurdjieff: A New Introduction to His Teaching* was privately printed. It arose as the result of my collaboration with Nicolas Tereshchenko.

Nicolas and I met in 1982 because of an article on Gurdjieff's teaching that he had written for an alchemical journal I happened to chance upon. We became friends and I learned that Nicolas had come in touch with the teaching in 1957. He was for many years in Jeanne de Salzmann's group of senior students at the Institut Gurdjieff in Paris. Jeanne de Salzmann was Gurdjieff's closest confidant during the last half of his life, and the principal exponent of his work from his passing in 1949 to her death in 1990.

Over the years as our friendship grew, I discovered that Nicolas Tereshchenko was at the time, arguably the world's foremost authority on Gurdjieff's great book, *Beelzebub's Tales to His Grandson*. As a native Russian/Ukrainian, he had studied the manuscript in one of its primary languages and later collaborated with Michel de Salzmann and others on the new Russian edition published in 2000.

My contact with the Gurdjieff Work dates back to 1978. I was told of the importance of Gurdjieff at that time by the man who would become my mentor, Sri Madhava Ashish (née Alexander Phipps), an Englishman who had become a Hindu monk and Indian guru. He explained that the inner or esoteric side of all spiritual/religious teaching is intended to help us expand our consciousness and through this to discover who we really are, what is our purpose, and what is the nature of reality. Gurdjieff, he said, brought anew the teaching to the West where it had been largely lost through distortion of western religious practices over the centuries. At his suggestion I joined a group of students in south Florida connected with the Gurdjieff Foundation of New York. Ashish's guidance, through his instructions and letters, strongly influenced my understanding of Gurdjieff's teaching, and many of his remarks have found their way into this book.

I had been in traditional Gurdjieff groups from 1978 until 1990, after which I found myself leading an independent group in south Florida. In giving introductory courses on Gurdjieff's teaching, I used whatever introductory texts were available, but never felt that they simply, yet adequately, introduced Gurdjieff's teaching to new people living in the contemporary society of the late twentieth century. As a result, Nicolas Tereshchenko and I worked together to produce a simple and straightforward introductory text. In working with that book over a number of years, I realized that a whole new text was needed. Experience with groups using the book showed its inadequacies in arrangement, suggested additional material that should have been included, and highlighted various errors.

Nicolas, living in Australia in recent years, had asked me on numerous occasions if I had begun work on the new text. In failing health, it was not something in which he could participate. The new text has now been written, and the result is the volume you hold in your hands. Through it I hope that you will be able to access Gurdjieff's teaching in a form that is simple, yet sufficiently comprehensive for you to judge its value in your own search for truth.

Nicolas Tereshchenko is no longer with us, having passed on in 2002. He was a product of mainstream life in the West, as am I. His career was as a British and Australian surgeon, mine was as an American lawyer and businessman. It is my hope now, as it was our hope then, that beginning with this book, the great benefit we have received from having come in touch with Gurdjieff's teaching can be received by others not dissimilar to us. That is, to that segment of mainstream humanity who are of a particular class that Gurdjieff called good householders. These are the people who have accepted the responsibilities that life has placed before them, but who nevertheless ask the penetrating questions about the purpose of life.

Those questions, sometimes called Gurdjieff's questions, can be asked in two parts: first, who am I, and second, what is the purpose of human life in general and of my life in particular? Gurdjieff's teaching reveals remarkable suggestions in answer to these questions.

These questions are addressed in the first lesson of this text, because unless the reader is someone who has been asking one or both of these questions in one form or another there is really no need for an inquiry into literature of this kind. Therefore, at the outset I have given my interpretation of Gurdjieff's suggested answers to these questions.

The earlier book was divided into five lessons whereas this book is presented as six lessons, an arrangement that experience has shown to be more useful.

It was the opinion of the authors of the previous book and it continues to be my view that if Gurdjieff's teaching is to have relevance for a wider humanity in the new millennium as I believe was his intent, students must be able to readily understand and engage in the primary elements of the Work. These are three: 1) working with a group engaged in practices to expand consciousness, 2) regular meditation, and 3) the study of Gurdjieff's primary text, *Beelzebub's Tales to His Grandson*.

Additional practices, especially sacred dance (the Gurdjieff Movements) and the so-called second line of work, the working with others usually in a physical activity in order to rub up against one another to observe our reactions and to act as self-consciousness reminders, are also important but perhaps not essential. At any rate, these practices require a larger number of people than what I regard as the three primary practices, which can be carried on by as few as two or three persons. The additional practices also require special physical facilities, which may not be available to someone approaching these ideas for the first time and who may not have access to a large already existing group. Consequently, they are not covered in detail in this text.

Every student has his or her subjective view of what Gurdjieff teaches, and so every work that attempts to comment on the teaching of a master is prejudiced by each student's level of understanding. Consequently, many students of Gurdjieff's teaching will not agree with some of the ideas put forward in this book. But unless a student makes his or her own interpretation, based upon what Gurdjieff actually wrote and the talks he gave, what one gets is the author's interpretation of what Gurdjieff taught. This is no less true of this book than of any other book that attempts to explain Gurdjieff's teaching.

Both I and my previous co-author, Nicolas Tereshchenko, felt that a new overview and introduction to Gurdjieff's teaching was needed if for no other reason than to more adequately reach a contemporary audience. This volume not only expands on material in the earlier book, but it introduces many new ideas with respect to Gurdjieff's teaching. Therefore, the responsibility for this interpretation lies with me.

We all stand on the shoulders of others who have gone before. In my case I stand, as it is said, on the shoulders of a giant, Sri Madhava Ashish, who is quoted throughout this book. Ashish honored Gurdjieff as a true master, as do I.

Prefatory material from the earlier book, *Gurdjieff: A New Introduction to His Teaching*, follows this preface. If Nicolas Tereshchenko, the co-author of that book, were still with us he would certainly have added much additional material, just as I have done to produce this new text. More than likely he would have corrected things other than those that I have corrected. If Nicolas were to have read this new text he undoubtedly would have disagreed with some of the statements in it, just as those living students, whose help I have acknowledged, have disagreed with one statement or another. In that sense, although Nicolas's footprints are all over this book, we cannot know if he would have endorsed it. I think, however, that he smiles upon it.

Acknowledging its shortcomings, I offer this book for whatever value it may serve you, the interested reader. In reading through the text, I know that you will not be fooled into believing any old thing, nor is any such belief asked. Just allow yourself a little credulity until you are able to verify the truths that Gurdjieff has set before us. I wish, then for you, that the light of truth this teaching contains will illumine your way.

Seymour B. Ginsburg
Delray Beach, Florida, 2004

From the preface to *Gurdjieff: A New Introduction to His Teaching*

Numerous attempts have been made to present a written introduction to Gurdjieff's teaching. Having been directly involved in Gurdjieff group work for many years, we are aware of the difficulties presented in such an undertaking ..Part of the difficulty is simply a matter of the passage of time: what might have been appropriate more than 50 years ago is now less useful because we live in a different time. Part of the difficulty is in trying to decide what to include in introductory material, as Gurdjieff brings so many new approaches to the hidden tradition. Part of the difficulty, we believe, has been the intentional avoidance of references to Gurdjieff's own writings in texts by various pupils attempting to explain Gurdjieff's teaching ...

We especially want to recognize the effort of P.D. Ouspensky, arguably Gurdjieff's most prominent and significant pupil, who produced an introduction to the teaching entitled *The Psychology of Man's Possible Evolution*. Over the years this book has been used more than any other to introduce people to the Gurdjieff Work. Ouspensky's more complete book, *In Search of the Miraculous*, has become almost the standard text of the Gurdjieff teaching. But neither of these works, nor any of the many others produced by well-meaning pupils, can substitute for the genuine article, and there is no reason to believe that this small introduction is of any more significance in approaching the teaching of a master. We simply offer it for whatever value it may have to the seeker.

We believe that Gurdjieff is no ordinary teacher but is, as he called many of the great teachers of humanity (although never himself), "a genuine messenger from above." We think that he was given a mission for the new millennium, and that mission was to bring the teaching in a form that could be practiced in the midst of life, the so-called Fourth Way. The ideas that Gurdjieff presents, really new restatements of an ancient and perennial wisdom, will become more generally recognized as they take root in the fabric of contemporary mostly urban society. This has already started to happen with studies of the psychology of types based on the enneagram, and with the use by business of Gurdjieffian techniques for motivation. It would be a pity, however, if we lose sight of the spiritual significance of Gurdjieff's teaching, and apply it only to better the mundane life.

There is a danger to the seeker who begins to approach Gurdjieff's teaching, and no preface to these ideas would be fair and complete without mentioning it. As his or her eyes begin to open and the seeker begins to wake up, it will no longer be possible to ever again completely close them or to go so completely back to sleep. Never being able to go completely back to sleep is a most beautiful but also a most demanding experience. Gurdjieff gives us this warning in the form of an aphorism:

> "Blessed is he who has a soul, blessed is he who has none, but woe and grief to him who has it in embryo." The Aphorisms, *Views from the Real World*, p. 283.

And again:

> "Blessed is he that hath a soul; blessed also is he that hath none; but grief and sorrow are to him that hath in himself its conception." Gurdjieff, *Beelzebub's Tales to His Grandson*, p. 246.

Seymour B. Ginsburg   *Nicolas Tereshchenko*
Fort Lauderdale, Florida, 1994   *Paris, France, 1994*

Sy Ginsburg in the Gurdjieff Study Group vegetable garden in Florida, November 1982. The Study Group house is in the rear.

Lesson 1

Who am I?

*And I say unto you, ask, and it shall be given you; seek, and you shall find;
knock, and it shall be opened unto you. For everyone that asks receives;
and he that seeks finds; and to him that knocks it shall be opened.*
(Luke, 11:9‑10) [1]

a. Gurdjieff: a historical note

George Ivanovich Gurdjieff (1866? ‑1949) was born of a Greek father and an Armenian mother at Gyumri (formerly Alexandropol) in what is now the independent republic of Armenia. His early years are shrouded in mystery, but involved extensive travel throughout Asia and North Africa before he appeared publicly in Moscow in 1912 and began to teach. He did not claim to teach anything new, but rather to restate ancient truth largely lost to contemporary societies.

Among Gurdjieff's earliest pupils was Piotr Demianovich (P.D.) Ouspensky, who was at that time widely known among the intelligentsia of Russia. His book on the higher dimensions of time, *Tertium Organum*, had caused a minor sensation upon its publication in 1912. Ouspensky became Gurdjieff's pupil in 1915, but would split from him after 8 years and go on independently to teach the Work, as Gurdjieff's teaching became known. An experienced writer and journalist, Ouspensky was the ideal pupil to explain the teaching in an organized fashion. This he did; his presentation of the Work teaching was privately circulated at first, and later published as *Fragments of an Unknown Teaching*. This title was later changed to *In Search of the Miraculous*. It was published in 1949 just before Gurdjieff's *Beelzebub's Tales to His Grandson*. The broader publication of the teaching of the Work through these two books took place only after the death of Ouspensky in 1947 and of Gurdjieff in 1949. *In Search of the Miraculous* remains today the most widely used text of Gurdjieff's teaching, and in it is revealed another name for the Work teaching: the Fourth Way. The Fourth Way (to immortality) is a way that is practiced in the midst of life, whereas the traditional ways, of which there are three, the physical, the emotional and the intellectual, have all required retreat into a secluded or monastic setting.

Gurdjieff himself gave the teaching out only piecemeal to his early pupils. This group fled Russia with Gurdjieff at the height of the Bolshevik revolution, going to

Constantinople (Istanbul) and eventually settling at a country estate known as the *Chateau du Prieuré des Basses Loges* near Fontainebleau outside Paris. Gurdjieff maintained a residential community at this site beginning in the autumn of 1922. Its eventual decline, beginning with injuries Gurdjieff suffered in an automobile accident in 1924, led to his closing the Prieuré to new pupils shortly thereafter, and eventually to his losing the property entirely in 1932. Gurdjieff, having moved to Paris, continued teaching small groups of pupils from the mid-1930s until his passing in 1949.

Beginning in 1924, Gurdjieff turned his energies to the writing down of his teaching, mainly in allegorical form through the overall title of *All and Everything*. The title *All and Everything* was intended by Gurdjieff to apply to what he called the three series of his writings, the principal one of which is the first series, *An Objectively Impartial Criticism of the Life of Man*, with the subtitle of *Beelzebub's Tales to His Grandson*. The title and subtitle were later reversed. Gurdjieff continually revised *Beelzebub's Tales to His Grandson*, based on the responses of pupils to whom chapters were read, almost until his death in 1949. These revisions were mostly designed to make the book more difficult to understand. Gurdjieff wanted his students to work to gain understanding, and not just have ideas handed to them. *Beelzebub's Tales to His Grandson* is considered Gurdjieff's masterpiece and is the key written expression of the Work.

The second series of the *All and Everything* trilogy is the book entitled *Meetings With Remarkable Men*. This is quasi-autobiographical, and by all accounts, an allegorical description by Gurdjieff of his life as a child and then as a young man. Gurdjieff wrote this as an adventure, recounting his travels in the search for hidden knowledge in Asia and northern Africa, which he brought forth later as his teaching.

Although Gurdjieff traveled widely in Asia and northern Africa, whether he actually undertook travels in the form described in the book is open to question. A hidden monastery supposedly at the center of the teaching has yet to be found, and at least two expeditions mounted by later students in pursuit of its location were unsuccessful. Some students have speculated that the teaching brought by Gurdjieff came from within him. This is in keeping with the tradition, described by Gurdjieff in *Beelzebub's Tales to His Grandson*, of the allegorical Ashiata Shiemash, whom he characterized as a "messenger sent from above." Such messengers, appearing from time to time in the history of humanity, have sometimes been the precursors of what later became known as a religion.

Unlike the seemingly impenetrable *Beelzebub's Tales to His Grandson*, *Meetings with Remarkable Men* is written in a straightforward, easily understandable manner. In 1979 it was made into a motion picture of the same name, produced and directed by students of Gurdjieff's teaching, including Peter Brook who directed the film.

The third series of the *All and Everything* trilogy is a book that appears to be incomplete but which was nevertheless published in 1976, through the efforts of Gurdjieff students, under the title, *Life is real only then, when "I am."* It contains several important exercises and a description by Gurdjieff of his great discovery of who he is. This is the "Who am 'I'?" that we each need to discover for ourselves.

The *All and Everything* trilogy, along with *Views from the Real World* (a collection of talks given by Gurdjieff), and Ouspensky's *In Search of the Miraculous*, are the principal written texts of Gurdjieff's work. *In Search of the Miraculous* is unique in the sense that the majority of it appears in quotation marks as Ouspensky's verbatim recollections of talks Gurdjieff gave to early groups. It is a very valuable and organized explanation of Gurdjieff's teaching, and far more detailed than this introductory text can offer. But one has to read *In Search of the Miraculous* with care, as there are places in it, appearing as quotations from Gurdjieff, which are at odds with what Gurdjieff actually wrote in *Beelzebub's Tales to His Grandson.* One suspects that these variances reflect both Ouspensky's level of understanding of some of Gurdjieff's ideas, which Gurdjieff cleared up in his own writings, and Ouspensky's personal views about certain types of people. Gurdjieff, in his own practice, excluded no serious seeker from receiving his teaching.

A more detailed biography and speculative hypothesis of who Gurdjieff really is appears in Appendix 1.

b. Sleeping humanity
Behind Gurdjieff's teaching lies the idea that human beings live and die in a state of sleep, but do not realize this. In this sense, all human beings are divided into two categories: those who realize they are asleep and who are attempting to awaken, and those who do not know. The idea that human beings live mostly in a kind of sleep state is not new. For example, we can find it expressed by Plato in his allegory of the Cave in *The Republic.* But Gurdjieff's teaching brings us methods about how to awaken from this "waking sleep," with all the freedom and cosmic benefit that this gives, because through the teaching we eventually awaken to who we are.

Because Gurdjieff's teaching is a "how to" teaching, it is directed at the category of human beings who realize they are asleep and who are attempting to awaken. For the category of human beings who do not know that they are asleep, there is no need for this teaching. It is only when a person begins to recognize the sleep of his mechanicalness and looks for a way to awaken that this teaching becomes relevant.

A primary feature of this state of sleep is the illusion that we are each separate from one another. In terms of our personalities, the aggregate of experience in this lifetime, this is true. Our personalities are each different from one another.

Another primary feature of this state of sleep is that we regard our personalities as real. By engaging in the method of the Gurdjieff Work, we come to realize over time that our personalities are not real in the absolute sense. They are temporal features that disintegrate with physical death or soon thereafter. Through the Work, we come to see that, in reality, we are not our personalities, even though our personalities are important. We are what Gurdjieff has called essence, our essential and imperishable being. In essence we are not separate from one another. In essence we are conjoined in identity with the universal.

This teaching then, is the "how to" hidden at the root of every religious tradition. It is the teaching about "how to" become more conscious and, by doing so, to discover who we really are. We shall examine the fundamental ideas of this "how to."

c. The verification of new ideas

Contained in this material are assertions that you will not be able to verify, at least not in the ordinary way that verification is understood. Therefore, it is necessary to state at the outset that it is not a good idea to accept anything merely because it is asserted. Indeed, a healthy dose of skepticism mixed with a reasonable amount of credulity is the best attitude for the student who comes across these ideas for the first time. Don't believe anything, but at the same time do not close yourself off to new ideas. Be open to them. Take them as hypotheses subject to your own personal verification.

Everything in our life is conditioned by our habits, by the few "rules" we learned as children; but Gurdjieff's teaching bring us many new ideas, many new possibilities. The aim here is to present them to you as well as is possible in an introductory text, and to help you to be a little more conscious of yourself during the studying of this material. Much more will be said about the technique suggested by Gurdjieff to help us become more conscious of ourselves. For now, just try to be aware of the physical sensation of your body as you proceed through the text.

Gurdjieff did not claim to bring anything new. When asked, he called his teaching "esoteric Christianity." But one will also find elements of Sufi teaching (esoteric Islam), Kabbalistic teaching (esoteric Judaism), Mindfulness teaching (esoteric Buddhism), and Advaitic teaching (esoteric Hinduism) embedded in what Gurdjieff taught. This is because the confidential or esoteric side of all religious teachings is the same. It is only on the exoteric side that they differ, because the exoteric side is the side of form, and in form they do differ.

All these esoteric teachings are ancient. In that sense Gurdjieff did not bring anything new. What he did bring was a restatement of truth embedded in these ancient traditions, but in a modern form comprehensible to 20th and 21st century humanity. In this sense, and for those who have not been exposed to esoteric teaching, these are new ideas.

It is necessary to hear about and receive new ideas; otherwise we can make no progress. But these ideas must be such that they can begin to offer us the possibility to choose our inner state, the state of our being, instead of continuing to be the slaves of our body, of our passions and of the opinions which come from sources other than our own thinking and reason. It is equally essential to be able to sense and to feel within, a "resonance," an inner response to such new ideas.

We no longer live in accord with our spiritual nature; in fact our entire life is based on opposite ideas which we take as normal. Hence, the question arises: "How can we receive new ideas?"

The "new" ideas may be of great value, but if we do not receive them in a new way, a way different from the one we are used to and which serves us to accept ordinary beliefs, then even the most revolutionary ideas will be immediately transformed and will become the same as our ordinary opinions. It is hard to change one's way of thinking and one's attitudes. We cannot choose how to think or feel. We think in the manner taught to us since birth. We feel as our emotions in reaction to external and internal circumstances compel us to feel. We can say that our thought pattern has been poisoned by what we call "a good education." Each one of us thinks by association in function of his habits and in accordance with a mental attitude copied from parents, relatives, teachers, and friends. In addition, we act responsibly and independently only rarely; most of our supposedly deliberate "actions" are, in fact, only reactions.

In our ordinary state, we do not think. In truth, what we call "our" thoughts come from outside and go through our mind, but do not arise from it. Thoughts do not originate in us, but to be true men and women, we should think by and for ourselves our own thoughts, and not submit to those coming from other, outside sources. Our age is the age of indoctrination. All the means of diffusion that surround us, newspapers, publicity posters, radio, television, the worldwide web, have as their primary aim: to convince us by all means to buy this item, to watch that show, to believe this opinion, to vote for such a political party, to admire a self-proclaimed "artist" and his work, to subscribe to such a newspaper or magazine, etc. In short, we are manipulated to react to outside stimuli rather than to act from within, from what Gurdjieff has called "objective conscience" or "objective consciousness."

Consequently, we consume without thinking and we believe what we are told we must believe. We have become the more or less consenting slaves of publicity and of propaganda, which seek to stop us having any inner freedom of thought, and to accept ready-made thoughts.

Without any doubt, the human psyche and thinking are becoming more and more automatic. Most people passively accept this bewitchment and are satisfied with being good "machines," set in motion by someone pushing their buttons and obeying each movement of the steering handles; or with being perfectly good puppets, without ever wondering who it is that pulls their strings and why. In consequence the "essence" of most people, the real being, falls asleep almost from birth and, receiving no suitable nourishment, fails to grow in the understanding of who it really is.

The great teacher, Jesus Christ, knew this very well when he said to his disciples: "Let the dead bury their dead." (Matthew, 8:22, Luke, 9:60)

If we want to avoid such a fate, we must ask ourselves the questions: How can we continue living in the world as it is, but without being entirely at its mercy? How can I think my own thoughts for myself? How can I choose my feelings and my behavior?

To become capable of resisting all the subliminal and other suggestions that assail us from all sides, we must be "watchful." We must be more present to our own individual thoughts. We must exert the greatest possible discrimination in accepting what we hear and see, and especially we must endeavor to be in the state that Gurdjieff calls "self-consciousness." To be able to discriminate properly and to think rightly, our own "I" must be present where and when the thought is.

To achieve this, that is, for our thinking to become freer than usual, more our own thought and less the thoughts blindly following formulas learned in childhood and coming from outside, we must begin by intentionally impeding our usual thought pattern. Then we will have a better discernment and, in a way, a more critical mind. Having a "critical mind" does not mean that our mind will be more encumbered by prejudices and more apt to refute or accept things without reason. It means that we will pay more attention to what we accept and to what we reject, and why. Thus, we become more free to think for ourselves. Therefore, in explaining Gurdjieff's teaching, the attempt is made to introduce several new ideas.

> We cannot guarantee that you will hear new ideas, that is, ideas you never heard before, from the start; but if you are patient you will very soon begin to notice them. And then we wish you not to miss them, and to try not to interpret them in the same old way. [2]

d. Who am I?

The question, who am I, has sometimes been called Gurdjieff's first question, and it is followed by the related second question: what is the purpose of human life?

It would be presumptuous to think that anyone, with finality, can answer these questions that have puzzled philosophers, theologians, and scientists throughout the ages. But

Gurdjieff suggests solutions and also gives us methods to work on ourselves in order to come to our own understanding of the answers to these questions.

In brief, we can say that mankind is faced with a problem of identity. We do not know who we are, where we came from, or why we are here. As we explore Gurdjieff's teaching, we are led to see that the root of the mystery lies at the root of our own being, somewhere in our awareness, in our consciousness. We discover that by becoming aware of our consciousness, we become more conscious; our self-consciousness becomes "real" and we "wake up." In "waking up" we experience our identity, the identity of the individual, with the universal. We discover that we can develop our capacity to perceive this identity.

The term "identity" is used here to describe the qualitative sameness of the human being and God, or the universal, or Endlessness in Gurdjieff's preferred terminology. In *Beelzebub's Tales to His Grandson*, Gurdjieff represents the creator of the universe as Endlessness. The term "Endlessness" is used to express God, or the universal, in both the sense of beingness (or, more accurately, beyond beingness), and also in the sense of the place of the universe itself. The difference, if any, is only in scale. This is very much different from the term "identification" as it is ordinarily used and which Gurdjieff called "one of our most terrible foes." "Identification" can be thought of as a false identity. The subject of ordinary "identification" and how to work toward freedom from it is taken up in Lesson 4. Becoming aware of our identity with the universal, and standing in that identity, is the ultimate purpose of the Work. The freeing of ourselves from everything with which we ordinarily identify and which keeps us from that awareness plays a major part in the teaching brought by Gurdjieff and gives a completely different meaning to the term "identity."

In the context of becoming aware of our identity with the universal, it is meaningless to say that any individual man or woman ever attains anything. Thus, the teaching is not about attainment, it is about the discovery or awareness of who we are.

> The spirit raises its human vehicle out of its own being and, through this vehicle, achieves knowledge both of the qualities it has made manifest to itself and of the undifferentiated and unmanifest being within which all qualities inhere. Our life is its life; our consciousness is its consciousness; our desire to live, to experience, and to know is its desire. [3]

In this sense we come to learn that we are "spirit" or, again using Gurdjieff's favored term, we are "Endlessness."

In the third series of the *All and Everything* trilogy, *Life is real only then, when "I am,"* Gurdjieff discloses his great discovery that he is Endlessness (God). This agrees with the same idea expressed in Hindu *Advaitism*, Islamic Sufism, and all other esoteric philosophies that recognize this truth. For this reason Gurdjieff called his teaching "esoteric Christianity." In Gurdjieff's words: "The difference between him and myself must lie only in scale." [4] This idea is also put forward in *Beelzebub's Tales to His Grandson*, where he tells us "the difference between each of them and our common great megalocosmos is only in scale." [5]

Whether, as Gurdjieff tells us, there is a difference only in scale, meaning that we are Endlessness varying in the scale of consciousness of our true nature, or whether, since we are images of God, as Gurdjieff also tells us, there remains some separation between each of us and Endlessness in full, is a question to which the answer will become clearer to the student as he or she becomes more conscious. [6]

e. What is the purpose of human life?

one of the new ideas that Gurdjieff's teaching presents to us is the term "Endlessness," or "Absolute," a term also favored by H.P. Blavatsky, founder of the Theosophical Society. Like Blavatsky and others faced with the problem of attempting to avoid preconceived notions by followers of the teaching, Gurdjieff wanted a term to describe the ineffable presence behind the creation of the universe. For this he used many descriptive names, most often containing the word "Endlessness," such as "Creator Endlessness," "All-Embracing Uni-Being Autocrat Endlessness," and 69 other such expressions.

Several words in English have been used interchangeably by students of Gurdjieff's teaching and similar teachings to represent the same idea, although scholars have attempted to describe subtle differences between these terms. These words, among others, include "Absolute," "All," "Endlessness," "Essence," "God," "Permanent 'I'," "Self," "Spirit," "Unity," "Universal," and "Universal Mind." The most common of these words is "God." It will not be used very often in this text because its historicity is such that for most of us it conjures up images such as that of an old man in a robe and long beard somewhere in the heavens.

The distinctive feature of all the images of God is that in some sense God is separate and apart from each of us. This is the opposite of Gurdjieff's teaching and of all parallel teachings that maintain the identity of the individual with the universal. Experiencing that identity has been called, by Gurdjieff, the fourth or objective state of consciousness, or the real world, or enlightenment. For the purpose of this text we will mainly use Gurdjieff's preferred word, "Endlessness," as a description of that identity.

Externally, Endlessness is unknowable. Internally, the more we know ourselves the more we know Endlessness because of that identity. Words cannot be used to describe the perception of identity of the individual with the universal. It is the subject of mystical experience that can be pointed to but is not otherwise describable. For the purpose of this introduction, it is sufficient to say that Endlessness brought the universe into existence, and that Endlessness is other than the old man with long beard and flowing white robes whom we preconceive as the God-like figure of the Judeo-Christian drama. We fail to understand the teaching that we are created in God's image, imagining instead a God "created" in our image. However, we can become more fully conscious as Endlessness when we become more conscious of ourselves, because Endlessness is our true nature. Blavatsky said there is only one life, and we are that life. Biblically, "In him we live and move and have our being" (Acts, 17:27–29).

In Gurdjieff's terminology, all the creatures made up of cells ("microcosmoses" in Gurdjieff's writings) that we consider to be alive and mobile are called "tetartocosmoses." On planet earth, at the pinnacle of these creations, the most developed tetartocosmos is the human being, whom Gurdjieff qualifies as a "three-brained" or "three-centered" being, that is, a being who has evolved and has achieved some development and control of his body, of his emotions, and of his thoughts. For the purpose of discussion, Gurdjieff generally uses the term "tetartocosmos" to represent a three-brained or human being. But what is a human being?

Here it is necessary to ask a question. It has been called Gurdjieff's second question, but it is a question that has been asked from time immemorial. At its simplest, the question is: What in general is the purpose of human life? This must be a burning question for each of us, otherwise we have no need of Gurdjieff's or any similar teaching. It would be presumptuous to think that we can come to a solution to this question that has so puzzled humanity in this introductory text, or even to clearly summarize Gurdjieff's proposed answer. But we can ponder Gurdjieff's suggestions.

Gurdjieff proposes as his answer that on earth, mankind is the only creature that can grow a "soul," which Endlessness can use to help with the purpose for which the universe (called "megalocosmos" by Gurdjieff) was created. Thus, we human beings have a purpose, and that purpose is to grow (or, as Gurdjieff prefers to call it, to "coat") within us a "higher-being body," by us called soul. But then we can reasonably ask, "Why is it important to grow a soul?

Gurdjieff goes into great detail in *Beelzebub's Tales to His Grandson*, in further developing the answer to this question. It is a question that has perplexed philosophers and theologians through the ages. What is important for us to appreciate in our attempt to understand the answer that Gurdjieff unfolds is that we are only relatively individual creatures. We are really part of the greater being called Endlessness, and we have the unique capability, as our consciousness increases, to stand more fully in our true nature as Endlessness. There is no qualitative difference between each human being and Endlessness. The only difference is that of scale or relativity, and as we become more conscious, the differences in scale become less.

In Gurdjieff's view Endlessness, whether seen as already perfect or not, needs the manifestation of the universe, and within that manifestation makes use on earth of human development represented by each of us, to become more conscious of itself. For this reason, Gurdjieff's teaching causes us to transfer our identity from the personality to the essential being that is beyond everyone and everything, to Endlessness. Through its "three-brained" creatures, including the individualized men and women on earth who have coated their own souls, Endlessness achieves the purpose of the creation. That purpose, the purpose for which Endlessness has brought the creation into manifestation, is expressed in the ancient commandment, "know thyself." In proposing his answer to this question, Gurdjieff goes further and suggests that human beings are an experiment on planet earth to serve as vehicles by which Endlessness can know or be conscious of itself. But how are we, as vehicles through which Endlessness manifests, able to know ourselves?

There is an esoteric Hindu myth which tells that before the manifestation of the universe there was only *Brahman*, another name for Endlessness. But *Brahman* was lonely. So, *Brahman* through its will, divided itself into three parts, known in Hinduism as the three principal forms of divinity, *Brahma* the creator or positive force, *Shiva* the destroyer or negative force, and *Vishnu* the preserver or reconciling force. We shall meet these three forces again in Gurdjieff's explanation of the laws of world-creation and world-maintenance. By the three parts of *Brahman* interacting with each other, *Brahman* comes to "know itself." This agrees with Gurdjieff's view of the need of Endlessness to know itself, to be conscious of itself, in infinite detail.

In theory, all tetartocosmoses can be vehicles by which Endlessness can know itself. Gurdjieff remarked that the ants and the bees were failed experiments in this respect, because they developed societies that were overwhelmingly mechanical and therefore impossible of self-consciousness. Gurdjieff saw mankind as an experiment in progress. To the extent that mankind remains mechanical, it will also be a failed experiment. To the extent that a sufficient number of human beings can become sufficiently self-conscious and therefore know the answer to the questions, who am I and what is the purpose of human life, the experiment succeeds.

f. Transferring our identity from personality to essence

In order to experience the highest state of human consciousness, objective consciousness, we must transfer our identity from the personality, which is what we mistakenly believe that we are, to essence, that which we really are. Because of our improper education or conditioning (Gurdjieff calls this our improper oskiano), we mistakenly believe that we are the personality. The personality is that tissue of memories, thoughts, emotions, and sensations that we have come mistakenly to call "I." Yet we know that none of this existed before birth and that all of this will dissolve at death or shortly thereafter. In this sense the personality is impermanent and thus in Gurdjieff's view, unreal. As long as we believe in the overwhelming importance of the personality we will never discover that which is real.

What then is real? Why, we are! We are real in our essential nature, that with which we came into this life. Gurdjieff has called this "essence." It is our essential nature, and from the state of self-consciousness, it must be identified in order for us to change our viewpoint.

Essence is what the human being brings into this lifetime. The personality, the "lower bodies," in its broadest terms includes the physical (and etheric) body, the emotional (astral) body, and the body of ordinary thought. These are the products of food, education, and experience in this lifetime. It is the personality or mask that we put on during this life. It is really Endlessness in the guise of each one of us that puts on the mask we call personality.

The change of viewpoint in transferring our identity from personality to essence helps us to understand that we consist of both essence and personality, but that in reality we are essence. Gurdjieff called this change of viewpoint *metanoia*, a Greek word which we can think of as a change in outlook. *Metanoia* takes place in us usually through many years of watchfulness or what Gurdjieff calls self-observation, in which we engage in exercises designed to help us to see that the personality is not really who we are and to shake us loose from this misconception.

We must not belittle the importance of the personality. Its development through food, education, and experience in this life is the stuff from which essence grows. So, our life, including all our experiences, is of the utmost importance. Through experience, our personality may be attracted to the esoteric influences with which life is seeded. When these influences accumulate in us, they form what Gurdjieff has called a kind of "magnetic center." This attracts more such influences and in this sense the Work finds us.

g. The Fourth Way

Many students of Gurdjieff's teaching regard him as an enlightened being who has undertaken a special mission designed to help contemporary people living mainly in urban environments far removed from the tranquility of earlier times. For this reason Gurdjieff called his mission "the Fourth Way," a way in life. Gurdjieff said that throughout history there have been three traditional ways that can lead a man or woman to immortality. By this he meant the transferring of our identity from the personality which exists in time and space and is therefore transient, to essence, which transcends time and space and is therefore immortal. These three traditional ways are: [7]

1.　The way of the fakir (the way of struggle with the physical body).

2.　The way of the monk (the way of faith, the emotional way).

3.　The way of the yogi (the way of knowledge, the way of mind).

Gurdjieff went on to say that historically, these three traditional ways were the only possible methods for the development of the human being's potential to be objectively conscious. Objective consciousness brings the recognition of one's immortality. It is the immortality of essence that is meant. There is no immortality of the personality.

These traditional ways have always required the person to leave his or her environment and enter into a secluded, monastic existence. But in the societies of the 20th and 21st centuries these ways are less and less practiced and are difficult to find. Gurdjieff brought a Fourth Way, a teaching that can be practiced in the midst of life. The primary significance of the Fourth Way is that it is a way in life, whereas the three traditional ways, even if they can be found, require a complete change in one's ordinary living circumstances from the outset. Through Gurdjieff's teaching, we can apply the methods he brings to the events of modern everyday life.

This teaching works on all three sides of our nature at once: on our physical body, on our emotions, and on our intellect. This is another characteristic of the Fourth Way. It requires that we become balanced individuals, using the events of life to attain that balance. As we become more balanced, we can be self-conscious more easily because we are less identified with our body, our thoughts, or our emotions. When we no longer identify with these features of temporal life, we discover that we are free of all fears and all desires. We then stand in essence, not in personality, and essence is immortal.

h. Beginning the quest

Having been introduced to the central theme of Gurdjieff's teaching, and having some idea now of what effort is involved in the pursuit of increased consciousness, we must ask ourselves two questions: "Am I able and is it useful for me to pursue such a quest?" and "If one begins this pursuit, can one withdraw from it at will at any time?"

Gurdjieff suggests we gain some perspective about what is ahead of us if we pursue the quest. He also adds a warning to the seeker who sets out on this way:

> Go out one clear starlit night to some open space and look up at the sky, at those millions of worlds over your head. Remember that perhaps on each one of them

swarm billions of beings similar to you or perhaps superior to you in their organization. Look at the Milky Way. The earth cannot even be called a grain of sand in this infinity …

Before all these worlds ask yourself what are your aims and hopes, your intentions and means of fulfilling them, the demands that may be made upon you and your preparedness to meet them.

A long and difficult journey is before you; you are preparing for a strange and unknown land …

Do not reckon on trying to come back. This experiment may cost you very dear. [8]

Why does Gurdjieff say that it may cost us very dear? It is because when our eyes are opened a bit through work with this teaching, we no longer sleep so soundly. Once being awakened, even if only a little, it may no longer be possible to return to complete sleep. We are warned by Gurdjieff that we are then in danger of being "between two stools." We have gotten off the stool of our waking sleep and we now realize the necessity of becoming conscious of our essential nature as Endlessness. But we have not yet reached the stool of being conscious of our essential nature. Until we actually stand in the unity of our essential nature, our position is much less happy than is that of the person who sleeps soundly and who is not reached by ideas of this kind.

i. An exercise in consciousness: putting ourselves in the other person's place

Because the Fourth Way is a way in life, it is practiced in the midst of life. Students of the teaching engage in inner exercises which need not be known to other people. Many exercises were given by Gurdjieff himself. Some have been created by students of the teaching. There is no need to distress others or call to their attention any sort of inner practice that may seem strange to them and even threatening. All such exercises have to do with the expansion of consciousness that is characteristic of the transfer of our identity from personality to essence.

An exercise that Gurdjieff emphasized more than any other is to strive to put oneself in the position of another being. It is a principal exercise and is among the most difficult exercises that he gave, but because it is so important let us try it. Take it as an inner exercise that we can practice in the midst of life. During this next week let us observe ourselves as we try whenever possible to put ourselves in the position of the people we encounter. Pick a particular person as the occasion presents itself, and try to satisfy what you perceive to be that person's wishes during the period of encounter, as if you were that person. Really try to put yourself in that person's position. At the beginning of the next lesson we shall share our experiences of what we have observed in attempting this exercise. Bring a specific example that you can share with others.

It is extraordinarily difficult to put ourselves in someone else's position, especially if that person is someone with whom we disagree. That is because we function through our personality, which we believe to be real, and each personality is separate from all other personalities. It is only when we stand in essence that we will be successful, because in essence we are all conjoined with the universal. Through the Work we begin to make a separation from the personality that we have been mis-educated to believe is who we are. In separating from the personality, we stand in essence, and we then experience what Gurdjieff calls genuine, impartial and non-egoistic love.

There is a particular method that is used for engaging in all such exercises. We must divide our attention so that all our attention does not flow into identification with personality characteristics. The method will be more fully described in the next lesson. The Gurdjieff method requires including the sensation of part or all of our body in our attention, as a device to help divide the attention. As we proceed through the week, encountering various people, let us try to have a sensation of our body including the sensation of its weight in our attention, while we attempt to put ourselves in the other person's position. This is the beginning of work on oneself.

Lesson 2

The expansion of consciousness

a. Selfobservation

The Gurdjieff Work requires that we engage in the ongoing exercise of self-observation. Self-observation is the chief means that is used to study oneself. By self-observation is meant the observation of the functions and characteristics of the human machine, the simple recording in one's mind of what is observed at the moment. We observe the human machine as we would any other machine, an instrument that can be probed and studied.

In order to properly observe the human machine we need to be in the state that Gurdjieff called "self-remembering" or "self-consciousness." This is a critical part of the process of expanding our consciousness and the inner effort required to enter into this state is explained in the remaining sections of this lesson.

During the past week, we have been trying to observe ourselves as we attempted to put ourselves in the position of another person with whom we disagreed. Let us consider these observations. What have we observed in ourselves?

b. Epanding consciousness

The Work is the development or expansion of our consciousness, especially the consciousness of ourself, and the Gurdjieff Work teaches us how to become really conscious and how to live here and now. We can say that Gurdjieff gives us the possibility to "wake up" and "to be" in the present. The Work is intended to help men and women to become more conscious and to acquire all the advantages and powers that self-consciousness brings. Indeed, the only real evolution, the evolution of which all esoteric teaching speaks, is the evolution of consciousness. Mechanical or Darwinian evolution only provides the vehicles or forms through which consciousness most effectively manifests itself.

What is surprising about consciousness, about the state of being "conscious," is that people believe that they are always conscious. We live in the certainty of being conscious, of being responsible for our actions and certain that others are also conscious and responsible. But in reality we are not conscious in the sense that we do not possess the consciousness of which the human being is capable.

Ask yourself: "What am I really conscious of?" "What am I conscious of at this precise moment?" "Am I conscious of myself while I read or listen to these words?" "What does 'am I conscious of myself' mean?"

You can see that it is not possible to answer these questions, not with words, at any rate. Perhaps these questions disturb you and make you think of the mystery that consciousness represents. But consciousness need not remain a mystery. We begin to understand consciousness and to expand consciousness by including the consciousness of ourselves in our attention.

What is extraordinary is that by becoming more conscious of myself, I realize that I know more about everything else, even about consciousness itself, which therefore becomes less and less a mystery.

Our question then becomes: "How can I become more conscious?" and especially: "How can I become more conscious of myself?"

It is even possible, if not probable, that by simply speaking about it, our consciousness of self and our general state of awareness becomes greater. But in the absence of a real desire to acquire, keep, and perfect a state of consciousness greater than ordinary consciousness, this state of expanded consciousness rapidly disappears. We do not usually live with that aim in mind and so we do not know what is the effort necessary to become and to remain more conscious. To strengthen one's consciousness and make it more durable, one must not only desire it, but also must try to find out how to act towards such a goal, what we must do to achieve the aim of acquiring, keeping, and perfecting the state of a greater consciousness.

The particular effort required is not known by people who feel neither the need nor the wish to be more conscious of who they are and to know why they live on this earth. To learn what this effort is, one must study and practice one or another of the many existing methods of self-development, the Work taught by Gurdjieff being one of the most practical and most effective.

This effort is not free and can be acquired only through hard and persistent labor. Consciousness cannot arise unconsciously! Make no mistake: those who pretend that consciousness can be acquired without any effort are deluding themselves.

There are people who claim that being in the presence of an enlightened being, one who already knows that he or she is Endlessness, can cause us to become more conscious. In India, this is known as receiving the *darshan* (the blessed presence) of the guru. There may be some truth in this, because what we see in such a person, the dazzling light of enlightenment, is that which we seek to discover in ourselves.

We may even resonate to the same vibrations as the enlightened being, and in that sense being in such a person's presence may give us a momentary experience of enlightenment, a reflection in us of what is apparent in the enlightened being. In that person is a reflection of what is deeply in us. But the experience is soon gone, because without our own effort to connect with our essence there is nothing permanent within us to remain enlightened.

However, what we call "effort" in ordinary everyday life is not sufficient. The inner effort to become more conscious must first be learned, then practiced. It requires a deep study of various subjects and a lot of hard work to follow and execute the instructions given by the system being followed. Only through methodical and persistent practice of the techniques can we expand our consciousness. Throughout this text we shall take up some of the techniques for human beings to become more conscious.

In ordinary life, we become conscious of ourselves only when we receive a "shock." If, for example, there is a loud noise, such as an explosion, we become very conscious of our presence and often a person in that state of enhanced awareness no longer acts as he or she usually does. He or she is temporarily liberated from inhibitions and mental paralysis. In these urgent circumstances he or she knows at once what must be done and acts rapidly, without hesitation. But real crises happen only rarely and so we remain unconscious during the greater part of our life.

If you are asked the question: "Are you conscious of yourself?" you will answer: "Yes, certainly," and it will be true, since the question has momentarily called you back to this consciousness of yourself, one of the technical terms for which is "self-remembering." For our purposes we can also use the terms "self-consciousness" or "self-awareness" to represent this state, although many students of Gurdjieff's teaching have attempted to make distinctions between these three terms. However, unless you know what the necessary inner effort is to remain in that state, it disappears as fast as it appeared.

c. The four states of human consciousness
To help us understand how widely human consciousness varies, Gurdjieff divided human consciousness into four possible states. In reality there are five possible states of consciousness for a human being (see Table 1, page 18). The lowest or least conscious state is the state of deep coma, a state of total unconsciousness. We often forget this state and speak of only the other four states. This is right in a way, since, strictly speaking, coma is not a state of consciousness.

The first state of consciousness, therefore, is the state that we usually call sleep, that is night sleep with dreams. The second is the state that follows the moment when we "wake up" in the morning. This state is called "waking consciousness," though in truth

Gurdjieff's description	Characteristics
4 Objective consciousness (enlightenment)	We experience the unitive vision and know we are the one life. This is called "enlightenment." It can be experienced but it cannot be described in words.
The Work here begins to come about naturally through effort from being in the state of self-consciousness.	The rest of the Work is to move from state #3 to state #4. Key elements of the "how to" are described as "Only he or she may enter (this state) who puts himself in the position of the other results of my labors," and "conscious labors and intentional suffering" (being-partkdolg-duty).
3 Self-consciousness (self-awareness)	We include ourself in our attention. (We divide our attention). We are aware of being aware of ourself.
This is the Work.	Most of the Work is the effort to move from state #2 to state #3. The "how to" taught by Gurdjieff is described by Ouspensky, as a double-headed arrow (page 19), along with examining the identifications that keep us from self-consciousness.
2 Relative consciousness (waking sleep)	Our ordinary "waking" state in which we walk the streets, write books, make love, and kill one another. We identify with everything that takes our attention.
1 Sleep	Ordinary night sleep in which we spend 1/4 to 1/3 of our life.
0 Coma	A state of profound unconsciousness.

Table 1 The four states of human consciousness
(to be read from the bottom up)

it is only a state of "waking sleep" since our dreams continue during the day, but we are not aware of this. Just as the stars are no longer visible after sunrise, but still continue to exist, so our dreams are no longer perceptible when we get up in the morning, but they do not stop, and we do not appreciate that we are still in a sleep state and still dreaming. It is the sleep and dream of all with which we identify, of all that takes our attention. Not only are we machines, but we are machines asleep. The intentional interpretation of dream symbolism is a different subject altogether. Its use by some students of Gurdjieff's teaching for the purpose of accessing the wisdom of our essential nature is taken up in Appendix 2.

How can we understand one another while we are in such a state? It is obvious that we do not really understand one another and no one even understands him or herself, because no one knows him or herself. We do not even know that we do not understand ourselves, let alone understand another. However, we believe that we do know ourselves and that others can understand us if they try. We blame them bitterly if they do not understand us. But they are unable to do so, just as we are equally unable to understand them.

The two other states of consciousness are accessible only to the person who has worked on himself or herself. Such a person is permanently self-conscious (the third state of consciousness) and can finally enter the fourth and highest, state of consciousness, called "objective consciousness" by Gurdjieff, and sometimes called by others "cosmic" consciousness or the "unitive vision." This is enlightenment.

The idea of the four states of consciousness gives what can be called a psychological road map of the Gurdjieff teaching. This teaching is referred to as "the Work" and most of this work is to move from the second state of consciousness called waking sleep to the third state of consciousness, to self-consciousness, by dividing the attention. About this, Gurdjieff said, "As long as a man [or woman] does not separate himself from himself he can achieve nothing and no one can help him." [9]

The remainder of the work and of equal importance is to enter into the fourth state of consciousness: objective consciousness or enlightenment. It is the state that gives the unitive vision, the experience in which we each know that we are Endlessness manifesting through each of our relatively individualized machines. In this state there is neither fear nor desire. But to enter the fourth state of human consciousness with any degree of permanence, we must already be functioning in the third state of consciousness.

d. The inner effort required for self-consciousness

The "how to" or inner effort necessary to experience the third state of human consciousness, that of self-consciousness, is the intentional effort to include ourselves in our attention. Ouspensky expressed this as dividing the attention, as follows:

> When I observe something, my attention is directed towards what I observe – a line with one arrowhead:
>
> I ————————> the observed phenomenon.
>
> When at the same time, I try to remember myself (be self-conscious), my attention is directed both towards the object observed and towards myself. A second arrow-head appears on the line:
>
> I <————————> the observed phenomenon. [10]

Our only tool for experiencing the state of self-consciousness is the intentional use of our attention, to divide the attention. Another way to view the intentional use of our attention is to look at the effort as including more in the attention. That "more" is the inclusion of ourselves in our attention at the same time that our attention includes all else that comes in through the senses and/or through memory.

Some students find it helpful to imagine an observing part of themselves somewhere near the ceiling gazing down and including themselves in the observation. But this technique should be taken only as a transitional aid to help in establishing the idea. In reality, there is no observing part of ourself because such a part would be in personality, and the personality is not real in the objective sense. There is only observation.

There is a subtle distinction between true self-remembering and illusory self-remembering. True self-remembering requires not only being aware of ourselves in our attention and at the same time including the internal or external object. It also means that we must be aware of being aware of ourselves in the moment. The object is relatively unimportant. What is important is to be aware of being aware. This subtle distinction may be expressed in the following manner:

> Observe an object. The object can be an external object like a candle or it can be an internal object like an emotional state: i.e. anxiety, fear, internal considering, desire, pride, vanity, etc. See the object. See what is seeing the object. Drop away the object. What is left is that you are seeing or observing what is seeing the object. In other words, you are aware of being aware. This is true self-remembering or self-awareness, avoiding the trap of illusory self-remembering. [11]

e. Attention

The inner effort that is necessary is best expressed in terms of attention. The person who really desires a new life, a new freedom, that is, an inner, durable change, has, in addition to his planetary body, the factory that supplies him or her with all the needed energies for work, only one tool: attention. The only effective tool to carry out the necessary work is attention. Most of the time our attention is completely taken by that with which we are identified. Something or someone constantly attracts, takes hold of, and retains our attention. Right now, it is held by what you are reading, but at least a part of your attention if you would experience self-consciousness must remain attached to yourself, to your presence here, to your activity now, at this moment.

In other words, you should be in the state that Gurdjieff called "self-remembering" or "self-consciousness" or "self-awareness." If you have forgotten that it is you who are reading this text and if you are reading mechanically without the awareness that it is you who are reading, where then is your sense of discrimination, your critical faculty? It is missing, as is the case most of the time.

Here is a critical and most important part of Gurdjieff's teaching, and the hidden teaching behind all spiritual traditions. It bears repeating and going over many times until it is fully understood. Being able to remain in this special state is extraordinarily difficult, but not impossible. It is this slim possibility, our ability to be aware of being aware of ourself, that is our only key to true freedom and our only means of access to the "higher worlds" of which all spiritual traditions speak.

f. An experiment in attention

Let us examine the work on attention. Here is a suggestion: let us try an experiment as we read or listen to the rest of this material. Place your attention on your right hand. If you accept what is suggested, accept it freely, choose to do it not because it is suggested, but because you have decided, of your own free will and accord, to do this experiment. You are quite free to accept or to refuse. If you choose to place your attention on your right hand, try to relax at the same time. If you have accepted to do this experiment, you have by now become conscious of a certain sensation in your hand. You sense your hand holding something, the book perhaps. Then you begin to sense the weight of your hand and you become conscious that it is attached to and is part of your body, that it is part of what you are used to calling "I." Remain relaxed and attentive and continue having the sensation in and of your hand while continuing to read or listen.

In your life also, in the midst of all your life activities, every time you remember, try not to forget to do it. Try to relax and to place your attention into some part of your body, thus becoming aware of the normal sensation which is always present in that part, but of which you are not usually conscious.

Because we dispose of only a limited amount of available energy, when it is used to consciously focus our attention, when we direct some of this attention to a body part while otherwise engaged, a lesser quantity of that energy will be available for mechanical reactions to surrounding events. Energy follows attention, so that although energy is used for attention to outside stimuli, a certain portion of energy is literally turned back within by including in our attention a part of ourselves as is suggested.

After what has just been said, the aim of this exercise is pretty clear. Through making the effort of keeping part of your attention on your right hand (or other body part chosen by you) you will not be as completely taken by what you are seeing or hearing or otherwise experiencing. You will no longer be completely subject to unconscious and unobserved dreams which pass through you. You will be a little freer from your ordinary state of identification.

You know now that you have a hand and that it has a specific sensation; this is a fact you are experiencing. And you are not as ready as you were previously to listen to your inner monologue about what you read or hear: "I have already read/heard this; it is rather old hat; how dumb can you be," and so on; or to lose your attention in something having nothing to do with what you read or hear: "I wonder if he/she really likes me? What are we having for dinner? That driver who cut me off was a real jerk," and so on. As long as you keep sensing your hand (rub your fingers together if that will help), your non-essential thoughts will have less force, will be less convincing, and will allow you to be more appreciative of the newness and importance of Gurdjieff's ideas, even if they seem to be already known or odd or ludicrous.

Now comes the question: how will you be able to maintain the consciousness of having a sensation of your hand? You have surely already realized that this sensation disappears after a few seconds and that you cannot sense your hand for very long before having to make a new intentional effort to bring your attention back to the hand. Every time you realize that you no longer sense your hand, do make the effort to sense it once again. You will often forget, for a varying length of time, perhaps even for days, to continue to make the necessary effort. You have already realized that? Very good: keep on trying, anyway. Why? To become more conscious of the existence of your body through direct experience of it and so that you may know that you have the power to direct and place your attention wherever you decide to do it. You do not have to let it wander uselessly, unconsciously and mechanically, lost in unimportant thoughts and/or emotions (feelings). If you let it do so, it is of your own choosing not because you cannot do otherwise. And now you know that consciousness can be obtained only through a voluntary, intentional and persistent action.

In trying to be conscious of ourself, every time we make the effort to be conscious, especially when we believe we are acting, we find that we do not really know what "action" is, because we almost never act: we react. We are incredibly passive: we only react, taking the easiest path. We are under the influence of external pressures, external stimuli. It is true, but there is nevertheless a possibility of voluntary, intentional action, because the only way we can act instead of react is through the voluntary, intentional control of our attention.

As we try the suggested experiment during the remainder of this lesson, let us notice what difference there is, if any, in whether we are acting with intention.

Much emphasis will be placed on experiments in dividing the attention as we proceed through these lessons. The work of dividing or including more, the "more" being ourselves, in our attention is of the utmost importance in the Work. It requires intentional effort to divide the attention and therefore to be in the third state of consciousness, the state in which we try to be always and everywhere. Meeting as a group is especially useful for this purpose since we act as reminders for each other. Group meetings should always include this purpose whether or not a specific experiment is being undertaken. Remember to use every group meeting as a reminder to engage in dividing the attention, using sensation of part or all of the body as a tool for this purpose.

g. Relativity of consciousness in seven different levels of human beings

It is suggested here that we are only relatively individual creatures since we are all conjoined in identity with the greater being that Gurdjieff has called Endlessness. It is further suggested that the only real evolution is the evolution of consciousness and that human consciousness can be divided into four distinct states, each relatively more conscious than the preceding state.

To help us further understand the relativity of consciousness, Gurdjieff divided human beings into seven categories of man/woman, each with its own level of consciousness. Let us look a little more closely at this arrangement to see if we can understand that there are vast differences between people depending upon how conscious they are.

Human being no. 7 is the one who has perfected him/herself through his/her own super-efforts. He/she has free will, objective consciousness, a permanent "I," and his/her own willpower. Therefore, he/she can do whatever he/she wants, and what he/she wants is always seen from and in the service of Endlessness, because *metanoia* has taken place in him/her and he/she experiences completely his/her identity with Endlessness. He/she is enlightened. He/she stands in the unitive vision. This is the perfect man or woman who is immortal, residing in the fourth state of consciousness. Gurdjieff makes a very interesting distinction between human being no. 7 and human being no. 6. The former resides permanently in the unitive vision and can no longer be deprived of or lose skills and powers.

Human being no. 6 is the one who really knows him/herself, is permanently in the state of self-consciousness, and has made contact with both higher centers, which therefore take part in all his/her functions. (We have touched upon the three centers generally familiar to everyone, the moving, emotional, and intellectual centers. Gurdjieff tells us that, in actuality, there are seven centers, including two higher centers, and this is the subject of the following section, "The seven centers.") Human being no. 6 has acquired all a man or woman can acquire: his/her individual "I," own will, "psychic" powers, etc., everything except permanence. He/she can still lose every-thing he/she has obtained through work and in that respect is not immortal.

23

Human being no. 5 has fully developed and properly equilibrated all his/her lower centers, and has established contact with one of his/her higher centers, the so-called higher "emotional" center. This man or woman is continuously in the state of self-consciousness, the state which we, ordinary "men" and "women," enter only sporadically, and then only if and when we apply ourselves to do the exercises that lead us toward it. Human being no. 5 has glimpses of the unitive vision.

Human being no. 4 is transitional. He/she has what Gurdjieff calls a magnetic center, having acquired a permanent center of gravity, knowing what he/she really wants and what he/she really needs. In other words, this man or woman has a well-defined aim and keeps it constantly in sight. Everything he/she does is in relation to this aim. The aim is to become more conscious, and he/she does what leads towards an expansion of consciousness, because he/she can choose what must be done. He/she has become capable of appreciating the real value of every "thing" in life because he/she is balanced. This is no longer either the physical, the emotional, or the intellectual man or woman, the type into which the human being was born. Man or woman no. 4 is balanced physically, emotionally, and intellectually. How does this human being and his/her further evolution into human being no. 5, then no. 6 and, finally, no. 7 come about? He/she is the product of continuous practical work on him/herself, very much along the lines of the practical exercises given throughout this text. It is a way of life. Through this work he/she has evolved from no. 1, no. 2, or no. 3, such as we are all born. Human being no. 4 is the product of work on him/herself.

Human being no. 1 the physical man or woman, no. 2 the emotional man or woman, and no. 3 the intellectual man or woman is every one of us, all on the same level, but of different types, reacting in radically different ways to the same stimuli. Each one of us is born into one or another of these three categories of man/woman. We are all born at the same basic level, with the same possibilities, but with different ways and capacities of perceiving and reacting to life events. From an objective point of view, none of us is born either "better" than or "superior" to the others. Nor is human being no. 3 superior to no. 1 or no. 2. Men and women nos. 1, 2, and 3 are all at the same level of consciousness.

h. The seven centers (brains)

Another Gurdjieffian concept that is connected to the seven different levels of human beings is that of "centers." Gurdjieff sometimes called these centers "brains," and he characterized all human beings as "three-brained beings." By this he meant that all human beings have an instinctive/moving brain or center, an emotional brain or center, and an intellectual brain or center. These three aspects of the human being, physical, emotional, and intellectual, are recognized in other psychological and religious systems. Sometimes they are referred to as the hand, the heart, and the head.

Gurdjieff further subdivided the instinctive-moving center into instinctive, moving and sexual centers, thus giving five centers. He also maintained that there were two additional centers existing but which usually go unrecognized.

Gurdjieff said that there are actually seven "centers," two of which are qualified as "higher" and five of which are called "lower." In every man and woman, there are two centers called the "higher emotional" and the "higher intellectual" centers. They are completely developed and have the capacity to function perfectly through human experience and maturity. In the ordinary man or woman, personality, consisting of the five lower centers, is not connected with essence, which consists of the two higher centers and which is our real being. Because of our improper education or conditioning, essence has been suppressed into the subconscious and takes no part in our ordinary lives. Thus, a principal goal of every esoteric school, including the Gurdjieff Work, is to help the student establish permanent connections between the lower centers (personality) and the higher centers (essence) in order to become a complete man or woman.

The five lower centers are called instinctive, moving, sex, passion or lower emotional, and thinking or lower intellectual. The instinctive-moving centers, including the sexual one, can be considered as usually working together in a single "action" or "instinctive-moving" center. The centers are likened to brains, and medical science today recognizes to some extent the localization of intelligence (brains) at various locations within the body. The instinctive-moving center is localized in the spinal column, the lower emotional center in the solar plexus, and the lower intellectual center is localized in the head. However, aspects of all centers appear throughout the body.

Human being no. 1 is the one in whom the instinctive-moving center predominates. This is the "physical" man or woman, the athlete, the soldier, the explorer, often the actor. He/she wants to be a champion, to play games, to climb mountains, to fight. For him/her, the body and its activities are the most important, feelings and thoughts taking second place in all decisions.

Human being no. 2 is the one in whom the passion/sentimental or lower emotional center predominates. For him/her, everything is subject to the demands of his/her passions, sentimentality, feelings and emotions, mostly "negative" ones at that. This is the human being who desires either a contemplative religious life as monk, nun, or priest, or an artistic life: painter, poet, etc. He/she wants to live in his/her inner passions, a life not requiring too much thought or physical exertion.

Human being no. 3 is the one in whom the thinking center predominates. This is the scientist, the scholar, the school teacher, or university professor. For him/her, it is the intellectual center's work that is most important. He/she uses mainly mental abilities and disregards or neglects his/her feelings and physical activities.

You can see now why there is not just one "man/woman" but seven "men/women." Knowing this, we can begin to understand why we cannot understand one another. Let us suppose we wanted to discuss politics or art or religion or even sport with someone, and speak about it seriously. We must ask ourselves: "whose politics are we talking about?" Is it the politics of human being no. 5 whose centers are balanced and who is capable of continuous self-consciousness? Or those of human being no. 2, the emotional, passionate, man/woman, liable to become a fanatic? Or of no. 1, the soldier who wants to fight it out rather than discuss it? Or of no. 3? All are politics and all are different.

The same applies to many other things, to religion, for example. The religion of human being no. 1 is not the religion of human being no. 2 or no. 3. Two people of different types can argue violently, thinking they disagree, when in fact their ways of looking at and of expressing the same thing is what really separates them. In contrast, it is also possible for two people to seem to agree, when they each have different objects in mind, but use the same words to refer to them. And this could lead later to mutual accusations of bad faith. If we take into consideration the differences in approach and language of the different categories of people, discussions would have less chance of degenerating and ending in acrimony, misunderstandings or violence.

i. Time

The subject of time plays a large part in Gurdjieff's cosmology. It is a subject that has perplexed philosophers and physicists. Many students of Gurdjieff's teaching have interested themselves in this subject and some, such as P.D. Ouspensky and Maurice Nicoll, have written treatises on the subject. Gurdjieff tells us that time in itself does not exist. At least it does not exist in the objective sense. It nevertheless plays a large role in all our lives. Gurdjieff suggests that we try to understand time in terms of relativity. He pointed out, for example, that an infinitesimally small world such as a drop of water contains a whole universe of beings. We know this to be true when we consider the bacteria and the even tinier entities that populate the drop of water. Time for them is relatively different than is time for us. Ouspensky tried to calculate the differences and concluded that the 24-hour lifetime of a large cell is equal to the 80-year lifetime of a human being. In this respect, time is subjective because the time of life for a cell is completely different than is the time of life for a human being.

For now we simply want to appreciate the relativity of time. Just as consciousness, as we have seen, is relatively different for different beings, so is time.

j. An exercise in consciousness: a "stop" before and during each meal

Because the Fourth Way is a way in life, a student of this way must make effort during his or her ordinary life to be more conscious as the events of the day and the week unfold. Here is an exercise in which we can engage during the forthcoming week, and which may help us to become more conscious, especially more conscious of ourselves. The exercise places a demand upon us to do this work. If we are studying this text as part of a group and are undertaking this exercise as a group, we are a group of people who have mutually agreed to undertake the exercise and to report their findings in a week. Notice that the group provides a "will" that we might otherwise not have if we were to undertake the exercise by ourself.

If you are reading this text by yourself, you can nevertheless engage in this exercise for the next week, noting your observations. Then read the next lesson at the end of the week.

The exercise, then, is that at the beginning of each of our daily meals (for most people these will be three in number), before plunging into the actual eating, we "stop" and again come back to the sensation of our right (or left) hand. We try to hold that sensation in our attention for as long as possible, even through the entire meal if that is possible. We sense also the utensils in our hand. In this way we will be self-conscious through some or all of the meal.

Some people, living together and engaged in the Work together, a husband and wife for example, have found it useful to remark "*bon appetit*" or some similar phrase at the start of a meal. This serves as a reminder both to the person making the remark and to the partner to be self-conscious. This can be done without it being unusually noticeable to others also at the table.

This reminder or "stop" is the esoteric reason for the tradition of "saying grace" or otherwise reciting a prayer at the beginning of a meal. These traditions were designed long ago as a kind of reminding or "stop" exercise as it is referred to in the Gurdjieff teaching. As is true of so many real teachings that have come down to us from long ago, the inevitable distortion of their real meaning over time has caused them to become merely mechanical practices, the true purpose of which has been lost to most of the current practitioners of prayer whether said at table or elsewhere.

Current practitioners of prayer, for the most part, offer prayers of petition. These cover an infinite variety of requests: everything from asking that our names be inscribed in the book of life for another year to requests for a new automobile or to be cured of cancer. All these kinds of petitions stress the permanence and objective reality of the personality, whereas the personality is not permanent nor is it objectively real. All these kinds of petitions request something of an entity outside us, but there is no such entity outside us because we ourselves are the manifestation in human form of that entity.

However, if we use the reciting of a prayer as a reminder in the moment and, as is suggested by Gurdjieff, we sense our body in that moment, we are able to use the tool of attention to include ourself in our consciousness. By so doing, we stop the mechanicalness of the machine for a moment or moments. In those moments we enter that higher state of consciousness, called here self-consciousness, where we are aware of being aware of ourselves.

Lesson 3

The transmutation of energy

a. A second experiment in attention

Let us begin this lesson by considering our observations during the week with regard to the Fourth Way exercise that we undertook as part of the second lesson. If you are reading this alone and not as part of a group, just consider how you did on the exercise. There were about 21 opportunities, based on three meals per day, to engage in the exercise. How many of those times did you remember to stop, to actually stop, and sense your right (or left) hand before beginning to eat and continue to sense it during the meal? Half the time? Very good! If not, or if you forgot to attempt the exercise altogether (and it happens frequently), this is also an important observation. It allows you to verify the state of your consciousness and the extent to which you have will over it.

Now, for the duration of this third lesson, let us engage again in another experiment in attention. Let us try an experiment as we read or listen to the rest of this material. This time, place your attention on your left leg. If you accept to do this, accept it freely. Choose to do it not because it is has been suggested to you, but because you have decided, of your own free will and accord, to do this experiment. You are quite free to accept or to refuse. If you choose to place your attention on your left leg, try to relax at the same time. If you have accepted to do this experiment, you have by now become conscious of a certain sensation in your leg. You sense your foot resting on the floor, the pressure of the surface of the chair on which you are seated against the back of your thigh, the contact of your clothing against the skin of your leg. Choose what you wish. Then you begin to sense its weight and you become conscious that it is attached to and is part of your body, that it is part of what you are used to calling "I." Remain relaxed and attentive, having the sensation in your left leg while continuing to read or listen.

To repeat: because we dispose of only a limited amount of available energy, when it is used to consciously focus our attention and we direct some of this attention to a body part while otherwise engaged, a lesser quantity of that energy will be available for mechanical reactions to surrounding events. Energy follows attention, so that although energy is used for attention to outside stimuli, a certain portion of energy is literally turned back within by including in our attention a part of ourself as is suggested.

This energy that has been reserved then becomes available for transmutation into finer substances. These fine substances are required for this Work, and their transmutation is the subject of this lesson.

b. The five being-obligolnian strivings

Gurdjieff's own writings include a special language. Some of the words of that language have been traced to one known language or another, others to combinations of words from different languages, and still others cannot be traced at all.

These special words from the language of objective consciousness are designed to have a specific effect on people. After one thoroughly surveys the new ideas brought by Gurdjieff, through the writings of Ouspensky and others, engaging Gurdjieff directly, as the student must ultimately do, brings a new understanding through direct communication with him by means of this objective language. This requires the study of *Beelzebub's Tales to His Grandson*.

Some of these words have already been mentioned. Two additional special words (obligolnian and martfotai) are introduced here as Gurdjieff's character Beelzebub describes the five being-obligolnian strivings through which a being who works consciously upon himself or herself in accordance with them, may reach objective consciousness. Several additional words of this special language will be introduced throughout this text. The five being-obligolnian strivings are:[12]

1. The first striving: to have in their ordinary being existence everything satisfying and really necessary for their planetary body.

2. The second striving: to have a constant and unflagging instinctive need for self-perfection in the sense of being.

3. The third: the conscious striving to know ever more and more concerning the laws of world-creation and world-maintenance.

4. The fourth: the striving from the beginning of their existence, to pay for their arising and their individuality as quickly as possible, in order afterwards to be free to lighten as much as possible the sorrow of our common father.

5. The fifth: the striving always to assist the most rapid perfecting of other beings, both those similar to oneself and those of other forms, up to the degree of the sacred martfotai that is up to the degree of self-individuality.

Gurdjieff gives much emphasis to these strivings in his writing. He said that many human beings of long ago who worked consciously upon themselves in accordance with these five strivings, quickly arrived at objective results.

In this lesson we take a closer look at the third conscious striving: to know ever more and more concerning the laws of world-creation and world-maintenance. The ideas presented may be difficult to comprehend because they deal with matters of a cosmic nature and are quasi-mathematical. But don't be intimidated. Try rather to get a "feel" for what is suggested in the text. These are ideas of a higher order, and although we might feel them emotionally to be correct, our ordinary intellect may not accept them. The ideas are to be taken seriously but not necessarily literally.

c. Relativity on a larger scale

Just as we compared the relativity of different levels of consciousness in men and women in the previous lesson, let us take another word, the word "world" and examine it. It is impossible in a few words to express or even mention the whole range of ideas that this word can trigger, but we can speak about a few of them. Let us be open also to the idea that just as there are different levels of consciousness amongst human beings, there may also be different levels of consciousness amongst large-scale cosmic bodies. The idea that a cosmic body such as the earth has consciousness may seem strange or ludicrous. Let us take it just as a hypothesis subject to verification.

What does "world" mean? What is the world in which we live and what is our place in it? We can first consider the world closest to us, the world of humankind. But humankind is only a part of the organic life on earth. So, for humankind, the world is this organic life or biosphere of which we are a part. This is our world. The biosphere on earth is a coating on the crust of the earth that belongs to the earth. It is within the Earth's sphere of influence. As we are part of the biosphere, the earth is our world.

But what is the world for this earth which is our world? Earth is one of the planets of our sun all belonging to the sun and, as such, the sun's family of planets of which the earth is a part, is our earth's world. What is the world for this family of planets? Its world is the gravitational and other influences of our sun, the solar system. And for this sun, what is its world? The galaxy, which we call the Milky Way, is its world. In it our sun occupies an unimportant place as a minor star near the galactic rim, far away from its center. The Milky Way itself is but one of a countless number of galaxies.

The world of our Milky Way galaxy consists of all the galaxies of which it is merely one. Then, coming to the ultimate conclusion, if we could but see the world of all the galaxies as one whole, this would be the one world, the universe (megalocosmos as Gurdjieff calls it), itself arising from and contained in Endlessness, the unknown center from which all creation originates. This megalocosmos, the universe including all its dimensions and levels of consciousness, is our real world.

In this teaching the whole universe is considered as an entity, that is, a living organism, in the same sense that a human being is a living organism, an entity. Our real world, the universe, is at least by hypothesis, a living being. We are so used to dead things, to dead ideas found in newspapers or statistics, that we cannot even appreciate the possibility that the stars are living beings. We do not consider that there may be an intelligence of stars different from that of planets. Such concepts are beyond us. We never think about our universe as a living being, created by the working of specific laws, a cosmos that is born, grows, develops, matures and becomes more or less conscious, exactly as a person is born, grows, develops, matures and becomes more or less conscious.

We think about the universe as an inanimate, inert object, a kind of gas in different states of condensation. And so we never try to establish any communication between us and our larger world. Yet we must become connected and communicate with this universe in which we live and move and have our being.

If we really wish to know and understand ourselves, we must first find our place in the universe. We cannot be studied in a void. We cannot study ourselves without reference to our capabilities, to our possibilities, to our different states of consciousness, nor without the capabilities, possibilities and states of consciousness of our universe. If we wish to study and comprehend the universe, we must begin by studying it in ourselves, because each man and woman is a universe, a cosmos, Endlessness, but on a different scale. This is the meaning of the expression you have likely heard that the human being is a microcosmos, a smaller reflection in scale of the macrocosmos, the name that Gurdjieff gives to our Milky Way galaxy. This is the meaning of the ancient Hermetic axiom: "As above, so below." In more esoterically exact terms, the name for a human being as given in *Beelzebub's Tales to His Grandson* is "tetartocosmos," and each human tetartocosmos has a sevenfold aspect within him or her, just as the great megalocosmos has its sevenfold aspect.

d. The ray of creation
The sevenfold relationship from Endlessness to the moon is known as our ray of creation. We can most easily see this in the gravitational relationship of astronomical bodies. There are an almost infinite number of rays of creation emanating from Endlessness. We are concerned with our ray of creation which can be shown as a chart (Table 2, page 33).

Considering both the relativity of gravitational control and the relativity of consciousness, Gurdjieff suggests that relativity can be stated in terms of what he called the number of orders of laws. By orders of laws he meant the level of the restrictiveness of freedom imposed upon each level of consciousness. Endlessness, for example, by this

	Astronomical name	Esoteric name	No. of orders of laws
World 1	Sun-Absolute (Endlessness)	Protocosmos	1 (3 in 1)
World 2	All worlds (all galaxies)	Megalocosmos (universe)	3
World 3	Milky Way galaxy	Macrocosmos	6
World 4	Sun	Deuterocosmos	12
World 5	All planets (as a group)	Mesocosmos	24
World 6	Earth	Tritocosmos	48
World 7	Moon	Tesserocosmos	96

Table 2: The ray of creation

method of analysis is completely free, limited by only one order of law, that law being only the will of Endlessness.

The restrictiveness at each level of consciousness imposed by the orders of laws derives from the addition of all the orders of laws on levels above a particular level plus the addition of three new orders of laws at any given level. In the chart above, our sun, for example, is restricted by twelve orders of laws: three imposed on the manifested universe by the nature of manifestation, plus six imposed on the Milky Way galaxy. The six imposed on the Milky Way galaxy include the three imposed on the manifested universe plus three new orders of laws imposed on the Milky Way galaxy itself. Then an additional three more orders of laws are imposed on the sun. So, in total, our sun is under twelve orders of laws: three plus six plus three.

The reason that, at each level of manifestation, three additional orders of laws of the restrictiveness of freedom are imposed is because the very structure of the manifested universe and everything within it is based on what Gurdjieff has called the two great laws of world-creation and world-maintenance. The study of these laws is long and penetrating. Therefore, the following explanation of these two great laws is necessarily abbreviated. The second of these two great laws is best explained first because it is the one with which we are most familiar. It is known as the law of the three forces or, using one of Gurdjieff's special words, the sacred triamazikamno. It derives from the initial dividing of the one order of law (the will of Endlessness) into three to bring the universe into manifestation, so that Endlessness may know itself by means of the manifestation.

e. The law of the three forces (the sacred triamazikamno)
All of us have experienced the law of the three forces, although most of us have never thought about it as a universal law, and our experience usually only shows us two of the three forces.

Both great fundamental laws of world-creation and world-maintenance begin to form the universe in Endlessness or the Sun-Absolute (the name given by Gurdjieff to the source from which all creation emanates, which we equate with the site of the "big bang"). Three noumenal forces are present there, and begin to unite and divide in accordance with their natures, obeying the reason for which they were created in the first place; and where they meet, they produce phenomena. These phenomena are the different cosmoses, the different worlds of our universe.

Traces of this law have come down to us from ancient times and are found expressed in allegorical terms through traditional religious teachings. In Christianity, for example, the three forces constituting this law are represented by the Father, the Son and the Holy Spirit. In Hinduism, we find them as *Brahma*, *Shiva* and *Vishnu*. The alchemists name them mercury, sulphur and salt. In Gurdjieff's teaching, these three forces are often called the affirming force, the denying force and the reconciling force.

In this overview of Gurdjieff's teaching we need to see only that these forces constitute the building blocks of the manifested universe. Most of us are familiar with only two of these forces, which we experience as opposites throughout the universe, sometimes calling it the law of opposites. Examples are positive and negative, male and female, etc. We are rarely aware of the third or reconciling force, which causes involution and evolution throughout the universe, although knowledge of this third force has come down to us allegorically in traditional religious teachings. The third force emanates from the will of Endlessness in order to be conscious of itself, and eventually to return to its primordial state of unity. This is the state in which it existed before bringing all the diversity that we experience due to the manifestation of the universe, but in full consciousness. Thus, the initial dividing of the unity of Endlessness into the three primordial forces as shown in the ray of creation, in Table 2, is the beginning of the process of gaining experience by which Endlessness becomes fully conscious of itself.

The third force serves its purpose first, to bring about the state of manifestation of the universe in which we experience opposites in everything. This is known as involution. Second, the third force serves its purpose to bring about the state of unity in which the opposites are merged back into one and the manifested universe with all its variety returns to unity. This is known as evolution.

We can think of this process as movement along a parabola. The "descending" arc of the parabola represents the "descent" of spirit, an infinitely rapid, vibratory state, which represents infinitely fine matter, into grosser and grosser states until at the bottom of the parabola there is an infinitely slow vibratory state, which represents infinitely dense matter. The return arc of the parabola represents just the opposite, the "ascent" of matter into spirit. It is sometimes called the path of return (to unity).

Gurdjieff called human beings, "third-force blind," and this is because the third force is a property of the real world, the world as seen from the standpoint of Endlessness in complete non-identification. The real world can be experienced only in the state of objective consciousness. It is the fourth state of consciousness, outlined in the previous lesson, of which we are not conscious but toward which we work. It is the state in which we are completely free of all identification.

In looking at the world from the standpoint of Endlessness we can begin to understand what Gurdjieff called the sacred being impulse of genuine love. Sometimes we have a glimpse of it in our ordinary sexual activities where there is a kind of merging of two opposite forces, male and female, and the participants in a moment of ecstasy, may momentarily experience the unitive vision, and with it, genuine love. But as Gurdjieff pointed out, this is like finding money in the street. It is only through long and difficult work on ourselves that we can become sufficiently detached from our personality to stand in our true nature and in so doing to experience genuine love.

f. The law of the octave (the sacred heptaparaparshinokh)
Accompanying the law of the three forces (the sacred triamazikamno) is the law of the octave (the sacred heptaparaparshinokh), which brings about all the diversity that we experience in the universe. It is the law which, by its structure, brings about intentional irregularity in the processes of involution and evolution in order to produce variety and experience.

As soon as the process of cosmic creation begins, having formed the first new cosmos, the three forces continue automatically making further cosmoses, in accordance with this first fundamental law, the law of the octave (the sacred heptaparaparshinokh). It is sometimes called the law of seven steps. This process of creation becomes mechanical and creates new, secondary orders of "laws" as well as new cosmoses, situated further and further away from the Sun-Absolute.

Because the seven steps or stages have been made intentionally uneven by the creative force behind the manifested universe, working in accordance with the two great laws of world-creation and world-maintenance, the wondrous multiformity that we observe, occurs. Some students like to think of this unevenness as hazard being built into the manifested universe.

The megalocosmos thus created is made up of a countless number of "rays of creation," each ray of which, in accordance with the sacred fundamental law of the octave or seven consecutive steps, has six cosmoses, each more distant from its parent Sun-Absolute. The first (proto) cosmos, is shared by all the rays of creation that issue from it. Each of these cosmoses is under the influence of an increasing number of secondary orders of laws which limit its possibilities and hinder its freedom.

The last world in each ray, its extremity, is a "bud" capable of evolving and of becoming a world subject to a lesser number of laws. In the ray of creation of which our earth is one of the cosmoses, this growing bud is our moon, the earth's satellite. Although some scientific theories assert that this is actually happening, other theories argue against it. Try to think of this process in the psychological terms that would apply to these cosmic bodies as if they are living organisms.

According to this teaching, the moon is not a dead thing, but a young living being, still a child, capable of growing to maturity if it receives the necessary nourishment, the right food for it to survive and develop normally. For this it is dependent on the terrestrial biosphere. The biosphere of earth produces vibrations from all organic life as this organic life dies and decays. If the moon continues to receive the right food of vibrations as it revolves around earth attracting earth's cast-off vibrations essential for its maturation, it will ultimately become a planet.

In the same way, every planet, if it receives the appropriate food, can become a sun, and so on along the ray of creation. In our own solar system, one of the planets, Jupiter, is speculated to be in the process of becoming a sun.

This seemingly peculiar teaching about the moon receiving vibrations from the decay of earth's organic life including human life is not unique to Gurdjieff's teaching. It appears in medieval and renaissance Gnosticism, and references to it can be found in the Vedas, the primordial Indian spiritual texts.[13]

g. The enneagram

Notwithstanding recent claims to the contrary and a spate of books primarily based on the psychology of nine personality types as used by psychologists, the strange symbol known as the "enneagram" or nine-pointed diagram (Greek *ennea* = nine), shown in Diagram 1 on page 37, was first introduced to the West by Gurdjieff in his earliest Moscow and St Petersburg groups in 1914. The primary purpose of the enneagram is to display graphically the working of the two great laws of world-creation and world-maintenance, the law of the three forces and the law of the octave.

It is a much more complex figure than may at first appear because, through its use, all processes and manifestations, psychological, psychical, and spiritual, as well as physical, can be described. Because everything in the manifested universe is constructed as the result of the working of the two great laws, the laws themselves can be found in the structure of all manifested things, physical, psychological, psychical, and spiritual.

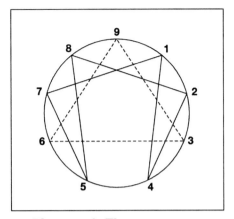

Diagram 1: The enneagram

Gurdjieff said: "The enneagram is the fundamental hieroglyph of a universal language which has as many different meanings as there are levels of men." [14]

The equilateral triangle within the circle, shown as a dotted line, is a representation of the law of the three forces, the sacred triamazikamno. The peculiar six-pointed figure also inscribed in the circle along with the triangle gives a representation of the law of the octave, the sacred heptaparaparshinokh.

The significance of interposing one figure (the triangle) upon the other (the six-pointed figure) is to show the three locations wherein the distances between the steps in the octave have intentionally been disharmonized. Gurdjieff labeled these distances, "stopinders." Using the musical octave simply as a device of convenience to help explain this, with do as the uppermost point in a descending (involutionary) octave or the lowermost point in an ascending (evolutionary) octave, these locations are between mi-fa, sol-la, and si-do. It is at these points in any process that additional energy must be introduced if we wish to act intentionally instead of reacting in our usual mechanical way. All our processes, those involving digestion and those involving attention, to name just two examples, are subject to these laws. Therefore, the Work that is fundamental to Gurdjieff's teaching is designed to enable us to introduce additional energies where and when they are needed. The enneagram, depicting as it does the great fundamental laws of world-creation and world-maintenance, is a subject for profound study as are the fundamental laws.

h. The human chemical or alchemical factory
Because we human beings are tetartocosmoses, we reflect microcosmically the macrocosmic structure of the astronomical universe. In this sense, we are our own miniature universe, because the fundamental laws of world-creation and world-

maintenance are everywhere the same. So, we have seven interpenetrating aspects, just as does the megalocosmos. In Theosophical teachings these are seen as seven interpenetrating bodies of increasingly finer matter. Other than the physical body that we can see, the six interpenetrating bodies are of such rarified matter as to be undetectable to most (but not all) human eyesight. The seven interpenetrating bodies, sometimes called the lower quaternary and the higher triad, are, in order of increasing states of fineness: 1) the physical, 2) the etheric (a kind of shadow of the physical), 3) the astral or emotional, and 4) the mental body. These four "lower" bodies are the product of this lifetime in which we each find ourselves. The three so-called "higher" bodies are: 5) the intuitive (often called "higher" mental body) and two further bodies, the Sanskrit words for which are 6) *buddhi* and 7) *atma*, but for which there is no exact English equivalent. We can think of the three "higher" bodies together in the term that Gurdjieff calls essence. Essence is that with which we come in at the beginning of this life.

Gurdjieff sometimes spoke in terms of seven bodies, but also referred to other systems that categorize these bodies as either three or four in number. The method of dividing them is only of intellectual significance in trying to describe our nature. What is of greater significance is first, to understand that these interpenetrating bodies exist only in ideal or potential. Crystallization (or coating, Gurdjieff's preferred term) of them is necessary if we wish to be more conscious, and for this to happen, transmuted energy is required. And second, to understand that the four "lower" bodies, the physical, the etheric, the emotional, and the lower mental, known collectively as the personality, are products of this lifetime and are therefore not permanent. The three "higher" bodies, intuitive, *buddhi* and *atma* are permanent and in that sense immortal.

Let us return to "man/woman" and our lack of consciousness. What must we do to become more conscious? The person who wishes to become more conscious must learn what to do in order not to waste all the energy his or her body can produce and transmute, and how to use part of this energy to become more conscious. Nature has made us as we are, with our many abilities. We can build bridges, wage war, make love, write poetry, compose music, walk on the moon. But if we want to develop ourselves and become free and independent individuals, if we want to have the power to choose our thoughts, our feelings, our sensations, if we want to acquire unity within ourselves and have a will of our own, then we must learn how to make and use energies higher than those needed for the life we live ordinarily.

We must process, in a special way, the three different categories of food which our body, our emotions, and our intellect need. For our body, the needed food is the ordinary kind we already eat, but which we must learn to take in and absorb differently. For our emotions, the right food is the air we breathe, and we must learn to breathe correctly so as to receive from the air the special rare elements destined for emotional development. For our intellect, the food is all the impressions perceived by all our senses. Instead of accepting all impressions indiscriminately, we must learn how to take in, and absorb in a particular way, those that bring us the special energy needed to expand our consciousness, to make possible the establishment of the connections with the higher centers, and to acquire our own permanent "I." Digestion, like all processes, functions in accordance with the two great laws of world-creation and world-maintenance. The enneagram of digestion (Diagram 2) shows

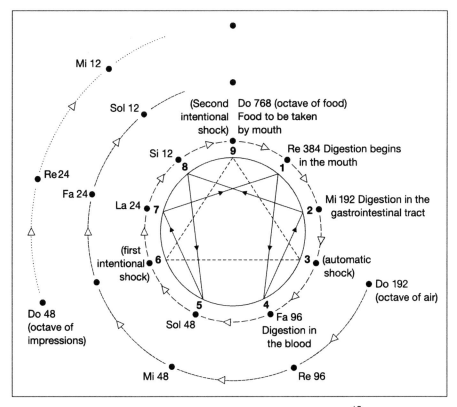

Diagram 2: The enneagram of digestion[15]

This shows the law of the three forces and the law of the octave in the processes of digesting food. The octave of air administers an automatic shock to the octave of food to facilitate its digestion. The octave of impressions, if taken in consciously, administers an intentional shock to both the octave of food and the octave of air to facilitate their digestion. A second intentional shock can be administered to the octave of food, the octave of air and the octave of impressions for both the purpose of procreation and the purpose of creating (or crystallizing or coating, using Gurdjieff's preferred terms) higher-being bodies. These are sometimes called the Kesdjan body and the spiritual body.

how each of the three categories of food must be taken into the organism in an appropriate place to maximize the transmutation of energies.

Our human body is a chemical or alchemical factory. It is a mechanism for the refinement and transmutation of the energies that it receives. We know from observing nature that each organism transforms the energies it receives, and in every case the finest energy, that resulting at the end of the food processing chain, is the sexual energy that is required to produce a new being.

Thus, the result of processing is sperm and egg (or their equivalents) which together generate new growth, a new body. In the human being energies are transmutable not only to create new external bodies as in procreation, but to coat new inner bodies for continued evolution beyond our planetary life.

This brief foray into the fundamental laws of world-creation and world-maintenance described by the enneagram as pictured in Diagram 2 (page 39), and the esoteric function of the human organism as a chemical factory for the transmutation of energies, is intended only to show the student the direction that esoteric study must take. It is a road map to be studied in very great detail when we immerse ourselves in the teaching. The Work itself is the treading of the path which this road map indicates, and this has largely to do with directly increasing the energy at our disposal for transmutation, and with plugging the holes by which energy leaks out of us.

i. An exercise in consciousness: a "stop" in the doorway

Here is another exercise in which we can engage in the midst of life, during the forthcoming week. During the week following the reading of this lesson, each time you pass through the front door of your home, physically stop while in the doorway and sense your left leg as you include it in your attention. Observe yourself: your sensations, your thoughts, your emotions, as you stand in the doorway. This stopping to self-observe is part of the process of disengaging from identification with the personality Always ask yourself the question in the moment: who is doing the observing? This leads toward recognition of our true nature.

This exercise is not new. The instructions for it are given in *The Old Testament*:

> And these words, that I command you this day, shall be upon your hearts ... and you shall write them upon the door-frames of your houses, and on your gates. (Deuteronomy, 6:4–9).

And what are these words? "The Lord is one." (Deuteronomy, 6:4).

Given the age of the text, it is remarkable that the instruction has survived more or less intact to this day. It is incorporated in the tradition in Judaism, following *The Old Testament* instruction, of installing a *Mezuzah* (container) on the door-frame of a home. In the container, along with other related text are these words: "The Lord is one." The meaning of this has become distorted for most contemporary people, who take the instruction to mean that there is only one Lord, a kind of ethereal Mister God, and not a cluster of idols. But the real meaning is that the Lord (God) is the one life, of which we are all manifestations, differing only in scale. The primary scale is the relativity of our consciousness.

Lesson 4

The conservation of energy

a. A third experiment in attention

Let us begin by considering our observations during the week with regard to the exercise that was given at the end of the last lesson. If you are reading this alone and not as part of a group, consider how you did on the exercise. Did you stop just for a moment as you passed through the front door of your home to sense your leg and include yourself in your attention. How many of those times did you remember to stop? Even once out of every five times would be very useful. If not, or if you forgot to attempt the exercise altogether (and it happens frequently), this is again an important observation. It allows you to verify the state of your consciousness and the extent to which you have will over it.

Now, for the duration of this fourth lesson, let us engage in another experiment in attention. This time place your attention on your face. If you accept to do this, accept it freely. Choose to do it not because it is has been suggested to you, but because you have decided, of your own free will and accord, to do this experiment. You are quite free to accept or to refuse. If you choose to place your attention on your face, at the same time try to relax, especially to relax the small muscles of the face. If you have chosen to do this experiment, you have immediately noticed sensation in your face because it is called to your attention. Hold the sensation of your face in your attention for as long as you can while exploring this lesson. Remain relaxed and attentive, including the sensation of your face in your attention while continuing to read or listen. If your attention to your face disappears even after just a few seconds this is not unusual. Suddenly you will remember this exercise and in that moment of remembering begin again to include the sensation of your face in your attention.

b. The importance of energy conservation

In the previous chapter we talked about the human chemical or alchemical factory, which is a mechanism for accumulating and transmuting energies for the coating of the inner bodies. We spoke of doing this directly by efficiently ingesting the three categories of nourishment that are available to us: 1) physical food and water, 2) air, and 3) incoming impressions. We spoke of the proper way to take in the most potent nourishment, incoming impressions, through the technique of dividing the attention to include both the awareness of ourselves and the impressions coming into our organism, either from outside through the senses or from our stored memories. In this sense, some of the energy that would be required to pay attention to the external stimuli is reserved for self-consciousness and provides an additional and very potent energy source that our organism can use for transmutation.

Also mentioned in the previous lesson is the need to stop the leaks through which energy continually pours out of our organism. This happens when most or all of our attention is attracted in identification to outside stimuli. Here, we shall take a closer look at this and see what can be done about it.

In addition to the continuous effort to be self-conscious, which aids in the transmutation of energies, the Work requires that we try to find out how the energies available leak from us, and how to plug these leaks. Our behavior during our ordinary state, the state of "waking sleep," leaks energy in many ways.

c. Identification

The common element that is present in the many ways in which energy leaks from us is identification. We do not realize that we are always identified. Our attention is always taken by something: by an idea, a person, a fear, a desire, by what we are doing or saying, or by what someone else is saying or doing. This identification is nothing other than an inner slavery. When we are in this state, and in ordinary life we are in this state most of the time, we are no longer ourselves. We are not normal men and women in the sense of having real will; we are really automatons controlled by external stimuli. We have no real will of our own, although we do not realize this. One can say that we cease to exist. If we want to be conscious, we must not be totally identified with anything. If we are totally identified, we are no longer conscious. This is why it is of the utmost importance to divide our attention so that we are not totally identified and so that the witnessing consciousness is present.

Gurdjieff spoke to Ouspensky and others about the evil of identification. He called it "one of our most terrible foes." He went on to say:

> It is necessary to see and to study identifying to its very roots in oneself … Identifying is the chief obstacle to self-remembering. A man who identifies with anything is unable to remember himself. In order to remember oneself it is necessary first of all not to identify … Freedom is first of all freedom from identification. [16]

We know from experience that it is impossible not to identify except for very brief moments. Our attention is always attracted to something or other, and it is that with which we are identified. For instance, you see something blue while passing a shop window, you like the color blue, you stop to have a better look. This is the first stage of attracted attention. You recognize that the blue thing is a coat. You continue looking at it, forgetting where you were going before you stopped to look; this is the second stage. Then, you like the coat so much that you go into the shop to examine it more closely and perhaps to try it on. This is the third stage. And finally, the fourth stage, in spite of its price, the fact that you have little money to spare and had no intention, when you set out, to buy anything, let alone an expensive coat, you purchase it. This is a general picture of the course of identification.

However, we also can verify that it is possible to divide the attention. So that even though a part of the attention is identified outwardly with whatever attracts it, the blue coat in the foregoing example, the remainder of the attention can be turned back inward for the purpose of self-consciousness, and Gurdjieff suggests that we sense the physical body in whole or in part as an aid for this purpose. It is in this way that we can become free from being totally identified. It is the dividing of the attention (or including ourself in our attention) that is the gateway to real freedom and to what Gurdjieff calls the real world.

d. The doctrine of "I"s and the role of "buffers"
One of the ways to observe identification in ourselves is to observe what Gurdjieff called all the little "I"s of which we consist. The major illusion we have regarding ourselves is that we are "one," a "unity;" that we have a permanent "I," an "I" who decides on and begins all our actions, and an "I" always responsible for our whole behavior. This belief is totally wrong. We are not a unity, we are a legion, an army of conflicting "I"s, each of which calls itself the whole. A coordinating "I" is missing in the man or woman as he/she is. Gurdjieff calls such a person a "man" or "woman" (in quotation marks) and, therefore, not a real person.

It is possible to acquire a real coordinating "I" in oneself, but only after special studies and through long and arduous work on self. "Man/woman" does not have a unique will directing all he or she does. Everything in "man/woman," each thought, each sensation, each passion, each movement, each manifestation, each emotion, each desire, each act, is the manifestation of one of these small "I"s. When a "man" says: "I am thirsty," "I shall be late," "I want to buy this book," "I hate this," "I want this cake," "I am in a hurry," "I like that," "I love you," "I do not like this man," "I shall kill him," etc., it is a different "I" who is speaking, and each one of these small "I"s is unknown to all the other small "I"s. They appear at random, called by exterior events onto the stage which is this life. Each one of these "I"s plays its habitual part in accordance with its type and the fragmentary, often wrong, education it received. When it is finished with its part, often only a minute or two, it disappears. Then another "I" appears and replaces it on the stage. This is the real portrait of "man/woman" as he or she is.

We all live under the impression that we are responsible, that we can tell the truth, that we can choose our actions, that we can keep our word, and that we are capable of doing this and that. But self-observation demonstrates that this is not so. All this is completely false, imagination, illusion. In the world of "men" and "women" (in quotation marks) no one does anything and no one can do anything. Everything happens in reaction to external stimuli.

How can we always tell the truth with all these "I"s we do not even know, and which do not know one another either, but each one of which rules us as the king or queen for a minute? Which one of these "I"s can really speak for us, in our name? One "I" says "Yes!" and another says "No!" One "I" says "I promise to do this!" but the one who replaces it does not even know what was promised and does something quite different. How can we, composed of so many "I"s as we are, choose? Who would do the choosing? It is not the whole of us who chooses, but an unknown "I."

The role of what are called "buffers" in the Work plays an important part in shutting off all these "I"s from each other so that we do not see the inner contradictions going on. The idea of buffers in the Work comes from the example of railroad cars which have cushioning devices attached to the ends of each car to lessen the shocks when they bang against one another.

Buffers are inevitable and important in every person because they are formed during the creation of personality, and personality is important to give the experience that human life requires. But if personality is not eventually made passive and subservient to essence, then the buffers normally created continue with the strong personality and prevent us from coming in touch with our real conscience.

Examples of buffers are all the justifications that an active personality puts forward to defend its importance. For example, I justify my angry reaction to the shop clerk or restaurant waiter whom I perceive as rude because they do not give me my due. Justifying my anger prevents me from putting myself in the other person's position.

The method of doing away with such a buffer is the dividing of the attention so that all my energy does not flow into identification with my angry reaction. The portion turned back within helps me to observe the situation dispassionately and to conserve energy. If anger is required to accomplish something, I can act as if angry. But if I am identified with the anger, then the buffer of self-justification remains and prevents me from seeing the real situation.

e. The "man/woman machine" and the terror of the situation
Because we have no permanent and controlling "I", we do not do anything that is directed from within, from what is our real conscience and which has been buried in

the subconscious. We mistakenly think that we "do," whereas in reality our actions are all reactions to external stimuli.

This is the horrible position of mankind: the "terror of the situation," as Gurdjieff calls it (see chapter 26 of *Beelzebub's Tales to His Grandson*). To know this helps in explaining a great number of contradictions and otherwise unexplainable and conflicting phenomena of human behavior. Each day we hear about suicides, murders, accidents, rapes, wars. How can such events be the product of human actions?

How could "responsible" people allow such things to happen? This is possible precisely because "man" or "woman" does not do anything from within. All our so-called doing is in reaction either to external stimuli or to stored memories. In this sense, Gurdjieff saw us as machines that are controlled from without, from external stimuli or memory that is stoked from without, and not from within.

Every machine is made for a specific use. There are many kinds of machines, from a simple hammer to a computer. We are a kind of complicated computer. The only difference is that we have the possibility of becoming something other than just a computer. But to do this, we must work and pay. Nothing is free in life.

First, we each must realize that, as we are, we are a machine, nothing more. As a machine, we are not our own master. If we never learn that we are only a machine, we cannot get to work to stop being a machine, to escape from the fate of remaining a machine all our life. If we do not become conscious of our slavery, if we do not become aware that we are at the mercy of these small "I"s, if we do not begin to observe them, to study them, to find their weak points and the way to get rid of the dangerous "I"s, how can we learn to harmonize them? Teach them? Regulate them? And finally master them and combine them into a single permanent "I?" Until then, any one of these small "I"s can, in 10 minutes, do enough harm for the "man" or "woman" to suffer the consequences of what was done and to be forced to expiate it for the rest of his or her life. Consider the example of a "man" or "woman" who in a moment of reaction, in a moment of "rage", "bravado," "lust," or "patriotism" commits the entire organism to an unnecessarily dangerous and lengthy enterprise or servitude. Commitment to military service or to marriage is an example of one small "I" having possibly committed the entire organism. Such is our situation, and we do not even know it. But it need not be our situation if, through work on ourselves, we develop a real will, a single, permanent, and controlling "I."

The first stage of the work of a "man" or "woman" who wishes to develop his or her consciousness is to become conscious of the existence of these "I"s, to observe them, to learn all about them, to get into contact with them. We must find out which of them are useful and which are dangerous: in other words, which of them waste energy and which act in a desirable fashion, or even in an absolutely essential way for our survival as an entity who can become a man or woman without quotation marks.

Do you see now the enormous advantage there is in knowing what is "man" or "woman" in quotation marks, in knowing it deeply and not only superficially, in knowing it in one's feelings and in one's body? Do you appreciate the immense power such a knowledge would give "man" or "woman?"

But what must we do with this power? What can we do? The power is here to become more conscious, to really "be." We cannot simply kill all the small "I"s. Many of them are not just there, but are absolutely essential, and in any case many others are deeply rooted and will remain, whatever we do. But in a person who is sufficiently conscious, these "I"s can no longer act as they please. They become obedient. Then it is a different picture. Our situation is no longer what it was before. We can change.

All identification uses energy, so that even if we identify with something pleasant, the desire, for example, to possess the blue coat, that is still a drain of energy. All identification can be classified as either a desire or a fear. Engaging in this Work, we observe the different kinds of desires and fears to which we have given labels, and we observe ourselves, making the effort to be self-conscious. This helps us to retain some of our energy that would otherwise be expelled through identification, and we transmute the energy retained into the finer substances necessary for the coating or crystallization of the higher-being bodies.

Categories of desires to which we have given labels include: avarice, bragging, conceit, gluttony, greed, lust, pompousness, pride, self-love, and vanity. There are many more. (See keyword list in Appendix 3.)

Categories of fear to which we have given labels include: anger, anxiety, hate, irritation, internal considering, lying, negative imagination, rage, self-importance, unnecessary talking. There are many more. (See keyword list in Appendix 3.)

Gurdjieff points out that the really heavy drains of energy are the drains that come from identifying with negative associations. These are all aspects of fear. He lumped all these into what he called "negative emotions" and said that it is imperative we do not identify with any of them and that we do not express them either inwardly or outwardly. There are many categories of negative emotions and within each category there are several different types. Let us turn our attention to examining a few of these categories, while at the same time including the awareness of ourself in our attention.

f. Lying

First, there is lying. Everyone lies and we all identify with our lies. We lie to others and to ourselves. Even when we want to, we cannot stop ourselves from lying. Does this statement seem strange to you? In the Work, to lie is to express not only what we know to be falsehoods, but also to make statements about matters we do not understand as if we do understand them. Gurdjieff calls this "wiseacring."

In ordinary life, small lies are often necessary and anyway seldom important. But in the Work, the lies we tell ourselves are the most harmful lies of all. Such are, particularly, the lies justifying our behavior. To see and convince ourselves of the truth of this, we must observe ourselves at all times. So let us not forget to remember that we must observe ourselves right now! But for best results we must observe ourselves in a special way. We must observe ourselves with our attention divided. Are you still aware of the sensation of your face included in your attention?

This lying is, at least partly, a consequence of our dispersion into many small "I"s and the impossibility of knowing which one of them speaks at any given moment. The "man/woman" in quotation marks is only a machine, a robot, controlled by external stimuli and by accidental events each of which triggers one of these "I"s. You meet a friend, she flatters you, you are happy. A little later she says something one of your "I"s considers to be offensive, and you are hurt. When your happy "I" is active, you speak at length with your friend and waste a lot of energy in small talk, believing this to be a good use of your time; when your other "I" is hurt, it sulks and thinks evil of your erstwhile friend. This also wastes energy, but you think you are right in feeling thus. This is a small picture based on our everyday life.

g. Unnecessary talking

A common way to waste energy is talking. We talk too much, constantly in fact, and not only to others, but to ourselves. We often talk not because we have something important to say, but simply for the sake of talking, to avoid the silence often felt as embarrassing, and by habit. Incessant talking is more often than not a manifestation of fear, fear of silence, fear of embarrassment, fear of insecurity, and so on.

Our small "I"s talk all the time, to everyone and about everything. If an "I" cannot find someone to talk to, it talks to itself. This internal talking continues every day the whole day and this endless, seldom interrupted, soliloquy wastes much energy. So, if I need a certain amount of energy to solve a problem, it is no longer available: I wasted it in talking and the problem remains unsolved. It is essential to learn to save and store one's energy and to keep it intact for when it is really needed.

h. Internal considering

Another frequent state unworthy of a human being is called "consideration." It is the state of being concerned by what others think of me, and especially of being unhappy about not receiving from others the admiration, love, etc. I think are due to me, this so very important personality whom I imagine I am. This is another type of inner slavery, another type of identification. I am tormented by what people think about me and by their behavior towards me. I am not given the credit I deserve. I am not respected enough. I have not received the answer I should have received. I have not gotten the job I applied for. I have not been noticed, and so on. So long as I am in that state, I am not free. I am conditioned by what I imagine others think or feel about me; yet, often, what I imagine is not at all what others really think.

This internal considering can be divided into two categories for the convenience of observation. On the one hand there is torment about what others think of me. On the other hand there is the making of accounts when I consider that others do not value me properly, respect me enough, etc. These are really two sides of the same coin, and we need to look at internal considering from both these aspects. In the one case I am worried about being embarrassed: "Am I dressed properly?" "Is my car nice enough?" "What will people think?" "Does what I say sound stupid?" In the other case I am indignant and offended by what I perceive people to think of me. "Let him/her wait, he/she is not important!" The other person may not be thinking this, but I perceive that he/she does. I consider inwardly. Do you see how both situations are alike? I am inwardly concerned with what someone else thinks about me, whether they do not value me sufficiently or whether I think that they think that I am not worthy of being properly valued.

So long as I mistakenly believe in the self-importance of being me, my personality, I will never stand in the unity of the real world.

i. Negative and idle (not constructive) imagination
Through this work I discover that I live in a fantasy world created by my imagination, influenced by my projection of others' imagined opinions. This is another drain of energy.

Usually, people think that imagination is admirable, a creative quality that should be encouraged. However, can a person who is not even conscious of him or herself create something worthwhile? Or even simply create? Although I think I am a "creator," I am only a machine. A thought enters my mind at one end and something containing that thought comes out at the other end. Did I create it? Imagination as fantasy is not healthy. Instead of being present to myself and my surroundings here and now, I imagine this or that and pat myself on the back as being "creative." Alternatively, in a state of negative imagination, a person can fear thousands of fantastic imaginary things, believing them to be real.

Fantasy imagination is not to be confused with insight, which occurs in all of us from time to time when the turning thoughts are quieted, whether unintentionally for brief moments or intentionally through meditation for longer periods of time. In the state of the quieted mind, insight from what Gurdjieff calls the "real world" has led humankind to profound discoveries.

Nor is fantasy imagination to be confused with intentional creative imagination usefully employed by a person who has divided the attention so that there is self-consciousness. In the state of self-consciousness, constructive imagination is possible. When we constructively imagine something that is objectively true, even if we do not yet experience it, the imagination of truth can bring it into our real experience.

j. Daydreaming

Related to negative imagination is daydreaming. We daydream all the time. We do not realize it but, behind our behavior, our talking and our reactions, our dreams are constantly unrolling, tingeing, and falsifying our perceptions of all the events around us. Daydreaming about negative things is a tremendous drain of energy, and intellectually we know this to be so. Since the motive for the kind of daydreaming that we call negative imagination lies in the emotional center, our intellect is often powerless to stop it.

However, daydreaming even about pleasant things is also a drain of energy, although we usually do not realize this, not even intellectually. In fact, we often consider the reverie of a pleasant daydream to be not only a harmless enjoyment, but a useful mental activity leading to creativity. It is nothing of the sort and is really just a kind of intellectual laziness that is very different from creative imagination.

Both negative and pleasant daydreams are leaks of energy, leaks that we must plug if we are to have sufficient energy for inner development. The method of plugging the leaks is, as always, to divide the attention. In doing so we become conscious of ourselves and can observe ourselves more objectively.

k. Identifying with and expressing negative emotions

The worst kind of the poor functioning of our machine is the expression of disagreeable, negative emotions. Everything disagreeable that happens to us causes us to express ourselves negatively: to complain, to have a tantrum, to sulk, to weep, or to show in some way the emotion, the passion that has seized us, often through imagination. We wish to go for a walk in the park, it begins to rain, and we are angry. We lost at the races, we are unhappy. We offer a gift to our wife or husband, it is not well received and we are irritated, hurt. We are furious. We identify with these negative emotions and this drains energy. When we express negativity inwardly, the drain is great. When we express it verbally, the energy drain is even greater.

l. Chief feature: our big button

Gurdjieff spoke often of "chief feature" or "chief fault," a central feature in the personality about which one's whole life revolves. It is usually the negative emotion with which we identify most strongly. It is difficult to determine whether we have just one or more than one chief feature. Gurdjieff talked about it as one, but other practitioners of the Work have seen in themselves more than one chief feature. Chief feature has been called our "big button," the pressing of which causes the strongest reaction by our organism. The more strongly we re-act, the less is our real will.

This feature is almost always the result of early childhood conditioning, and for this reason it is, as Gurdjieff says, "necessary to see and to study identifying to its very roots in oneself." The psychological self-examination necessary to discover one's chief feature is a long-term process, and the nature of our chief feature is difficult to discover without outside help.

The study of our dreams for the meaning of symbols exposed in dream stories is an important aid in discovering our chief feature. While the outside help of a trusted advisor can be of benefit in discovering chief feature, the Work is always one's own work, and we can ourselves learn the language of dreams and how to work with them to uncover their meaning. For a more complete discussion of dreams as a tool to help in work on oneself, see Appendix 2, "Gurdjieff and the Study of Dreams."

The identification involved in inner and outer lying, unnecessary inner and outer talking, attracted attention, internal considering, idle and negative imagination, identification with and expression of negative emotions, and daydreaming are all categories of the many ways through which we waste our vital energies, depriving ourselves of the greater part of our strength. There are many more categories of identification, and chief feature(s) is the strongest of all our identifications All are the disastrous results of the poor functioning of our machine. All this dissipates enormous amounts of energy, to the detriment of things of greater value. This is the result of our mechanicalness.

When we perceive this truth, we can begin to understand why nothing goes right in our world. Such is our inner world, the fantastic dream world in which we live without even knowing it and therefore without taking these phenomena into account. On this is what we base that which we call our "actions." It is the world of our inner slavery. However, we can get out of it as we find the means to know ourselves and to become more conscious.

m. External considering

The opposite of internal considering is external considering. Not only is it exactly the opposite of internal considering, it is something that is not accessible to us in our usual state of identification with some aspect of our personality. It is only when we are in the third state of consciousness, self-consciousness, and aware of being aware of ourselves that we can begin to approach external considering, because it requires a detachment from identification.

External considering is literally putting oneself in the other person's shoes. It is entering into the position of another in such a way that we are really able to understand and feel what another person thinks and feels. It is the stuff of which saints are made. This does not mean that it is a state not possible for us, for what we are after in this Work is something very big.

We all know saints. They are not only the beatified figures of our history books; they are the everyday saintly people who, if we are fortunate, make themselves known to us. Putting ourselves in the other person's shoes is a state toward which we strive using the teaching of the Work.

In *Beelzebub's Tales to His Grandson*, Gurdjieff speaks of the "Holy Planet Purgatory." He explains purgatory not as some ambiguous half-way house between the heaven and hell of the Christian myth. It is rather a special state accessible to those who engage in the Work intentionally and is part of the process of becoming conscious in the way about which Gurdjieff speaks of consciousness. The "Holy Planet Purgatory" is the highest state of human consciousness. It is the state entered into by those who, in Gurdjieff's terms, have already coated their highest-being body. Engraved over the chief entrance of the "Holy Planet Purgatory," Gurdjieff tells us, are the words: "ONLY HE MAY ENTER HERE WHO PUTS HIMSELF IN THE POSITION OF THE OTHER RESULTS OF MY LABORS." [17]

n. An exercise in consciousness: internal considering

During this next week, as a Fourth-Way exercise, let us look at one of the categories of identification that drain us of energy, the category of "internal considering." When you go into a supermarket or restaurant, notice your impatience with the slowness of the service, the uncaring attitude of the assistants, the lack of the merchandise or food for which you came, any of the other irritations that are commonly found in this situation. Or, when you are working, the rudeness of your clients or customers. Observe yourself and the thoughts and emotions that are going through you: "How dare they treat me this way, I am an important customer and I am not being given my due," or "I am doing my best to help these people and they are abusing me," or similar thoughts and emotions. This is internal considering. Observe it. Divide your attention so that the experience of yourself is included in your attention at the same time as the negative emotion of internal considering is included in your attention. See what happens. Does the effort of Work ameliorate the negativity and if so, can you verify that energy is being retained?

Lesson 5

Meditation

a. First, a look at internal considering

Let us begin by examining our observations during the week with regard to the exercise that was given at the end of the fourth lesson. If you are reading this alone and not as part of a group, just think about how you did on the exercise. Were you able to observe yourself in the moments of internal considering? If you were, did you notice that because you divided your attention you were not so negatively identified with whatever aspects of internal considering you observed? Did you feel quite so offended by the assistant in the shop or restaurant who did not help you, or by your client who abused you? Part of your attention was employed to include yourself in the experience and a part of you was observing the whole scene.

Can you understand what Gurdjieff meant when he said that as long as a man or woman does not separate himself from himself he can achieve nothing and no one can help him? You have already begun to separate yourself from yourself. You have begun the process of freeing yourself from the tyranny of the false belief in the permanence and objective reality of your personality

Remember again that if you forgot to attempt the exercise altogether, this is also an important observation. It allows you to verify the state of your consciousness and the extent to which you have will over it.

As we read this fifth lesson let us try to include a global sensation of our entire body in our attention. The technique will be explained more fully as we examine the Gurdjieffian meditation technique. Remember that this technique requires including sensation in the attention. It begins with a thought but then moves to sensation of the physical body, part by part.

b. The theory of esotericism

The theory of esotericism and the implied necessity for meditation was explained by Gurdjieff this way:

> The theory of esotericism is that mankind consists of two circles: a large outer circle, embracing all human beings, and a small circle of instructed and understanding

people at the center. Real instruction, which alone can change us, can only come from this center, and the aim of this teaching is to help us to prepare ourselves to receive such instruction. [18]

In meditation, when we have sufficiently observed ourself and been able to separate ourself from ourself through the techniques of the Work, we are able to sit quietly, devoid of ordinary thought and ordinary emotion. This is the preparation to which Gurdjieff refers. In this quiet state, real instruction from the inner planes of the psyche can be received. Whether this instruction is seen as intuition or insight, coming from a higher part of ourselves, the higher intellectual center or the higher emotional center about which Gurdjieff spoke, or from some discreet intelligence of which we are part and to which we have given a label, is secondary. It is this instruction to which Gurdjieff referred in his reply, quoted above, to a question asked of him in 1922.

The meditative state, when all other conditions are met, provides the ground for the unitive vision. This is the vision of seers who have the overwhelming and wordless experience of the unity of all being with its freedom from all fears and desires.

c. Gurdjieffian meditation

"Meditation" is one of those words that means different things to different people. There are many practices that pass for meditation. Here, meditation is taken to be a specific practice that presumably was introduced into group work by Gurdjieff's close confidant, Jeanne de Salzmann. In the Gurdjieff tradition it is sometimes called the "morning sitting" or the "morning preparation" or simply "sitting."

Gurdjieff himself suggested meditation in particular contexts to particular persons. But exactly what techniques he suggested would have been known only to those persons. However, Gurdjieff describes the quality of the state of meditation in this way:

And only, when, thereafter, I had finally attained complete freedom from all the bodily and spiritual associations of ordinary life, I began to meditate how to be. [19]

What is understood today as Gurdjieffian meditation is the sitting technique that is given by way of demonstration in groups. It is not a unique technique and is similar, for example, to the Hindu meditative practice known as *nidra yoga* meditation and the Buddhist meditative practice known as *vipassana* meditation. This is a meditative technique that centers around using our attention to include in it the sensation of our physical body in order to avoid all our attention being taken away by turning thoughts and emotions. Meditation of this kind leads to a freedom or detachment from identification with the physical body, and as the turning thoughts and emotions quiet down, to a detachment from them as well and to a vacuity from thoughts and emotions. Features of this particular meditative technique include the following, which will be described in further detail:

1. Inclusion of a global sensation of the body in the attention, including the breath.

2. Absolute silence: There is no chanting, talking, or listening to music.

3. The eyes are kept closed. There is not the so-called "soft eyes" condition of slightly open eyes.

4. There is no visualization.

5. There is no attention given to a so-called "seed thought."

6. There is no demand for any particularly rigid or unmoving posture. What is sought is a position that is sufficiently comfortable to allow sitting quietly for an extended period of time without falling asleep.

What we are attempting in meditation is to arrive at a very quiet place where there is not even a fleeting thought that stands in the way of our perception. It is in this extreme quiet, when the attention is taken by neither ordinary thought nor ordinary emotion, that the window of vision clears. In this clarity, call it insight if you like, we may experience the unitive vision, another name for enlightenment, or in the Gurdjieffian terms, "objective consciousness" and the "real world."

> In the unitive vision the identity of the individual with the universal is experienced, and it is perceived that this identity encompasses all being as an eternally valid fact. It has not come into being with the seer's attainment to the vision, but simply is. What comes into being, or, more truly, is developed in the seer, is the seer's capacity to perceive the identity. In this context it seems meaningless to say that any individual man ever attains anything. The spirit raises its human vehicle out of its own being and, through this vehicle, achieves knowledge both of the qualities it has made manifest to itself and of the undifferentiated and unmanifest being within which all qualities inhere. Our life is its life; our awareness is its awareness; our desire to live, to experience, and to know, is its desire. [20]

d. Preparation

Understanding the primary importance of meditation in the Work, we shall want to look at some preliminary considerations in preparation for our periods of quiet sitting.

The meditative techniques suggested here presuppose that we have some experience with "sitting quietly." But if we do not, now is the time to begin to gain this experience. We should regard the meditative period as the most important part of our day. It is a time that we have intentionally given over to something else, a "something" that we may not as yet understand, but which we know is completely separate and apart from our ordinary life activities. Customarily, the primary time period to be given over to meditation is about one hour, although we should regard it as un-termed. The actual period of sitting within the hour is more likely to be 30–50 minutes, although some people will sit for well over an hour. The meditation period must be sufficiently long and unencumbered by things we must do afterward, so that we do not find ourselves concerned about time constraints while we sit. Many practitioners have found that it is necessary to sit quietly for at least 20 minutes to arrive at a place of sufficient quietude so that the turning thoughts and ordinary emotions will have ceased, and a vacuity is experienced in the moments before a new thought arises.

In addition to the primary meditation period, one or two shorter quiet times during the day will prove useful. Sometimes, as a self-imposed exercise, the exact timing of these quiet times may be determined during the morning preparation. Such periods are then called, "appointments with oneself."

The customary primary meditation time is early morning. The advantage of this time is that the mind has not yet filled up with thoughts related to the events of the day. However, some practitioners have found it more useful to have the primary meditation period either in late afternoon or at night after the work and events of the day have been completed. The advantage here is that there is less demand on the attention for what one must get done during the day.

Obviously, if we can engage in two primary meditation periods, this will further enhance our work on self. But we should remember that this teaching is the Fourth Way, a way in life, not in a monastery, so we have to engage in meditative practice within the time constraints of our ordinary life. We each need to find the time period or periods that work best, and we should not be reluctant to experiment.

It is important that the meditation period becomes a regular, natural and primary part of our existence. At the outset, 15 minutes of sitting daily is much preferable to sitting for 2 hours once each week. Even if 15 minutes of sitting is insufficient to arrive at true quiet, it is the primacy of at least one daily appointment that is most important. If we are new to meditation, we must realize that this demand to make the sitting period a primary part of our day will not come easily. But if we stick with our resolve, a change in us will occur over time, so that meditation does become regular, natural and primary.

There should be a special place set aside in our home where meditation is usually done. A special room is good if it is available, but just the same corner of a room used for other purposes is quite satisfactory. The pillow or seat should likewise be special, the same one being used regularly. It has been asserted that we create an atmosphere of unique vibrations around us and that these vibrations remain near to our regular location. Even if this cannot be verified, whatever we can do to make the experience primary and of importance, like using a special place and/or a special pillow," adds to the primacy.

The lotus seat, half lotus seat, kneeling and sitting back on the heels, or simply sitting cross-legged are the preferable postures, although sitting in a straight-backed chair with both feet on the floor is satisfactory if one cannot accommodate sitting on a cushion on the floor. The advantage of the lotus seat, half lotus seat, or simple cross-legged position is that it concentrates the size of our organism and, in turn, our energy, making it easier to include the entire experience of ourself in our attention. Usually, our hands will be cupped together in our lap. Sitting in a straight-backed chair with hands on our thighs, also known as the Egyptian position, often works better for people who are too discomfited by sitting cross-legged. In any position, the spine should be held reasonably perpendicular to the center of the earth. This facilitates the movement of energy through the body. Adequate comfort that permits a lengthy period of sitting is preferred to a rigid, uncomfortable posture.

The meditative technique that will be introduced here is a device for intentionally deepening the experience of the third state of consciousness, called by Gurdjieff self-consciousness, or self-awareness, or self-remembering. The frequent and prolonged experience of this state in waking life while making our ordinary rounds is helpful to us in entering into this kind of meditation when we sit quietly. Therefore, regular work on ourselves to be self-conscious during our ordinary life activities prepares us for the deep meditative experience in which we wish to engage. Conversely, regularly engaging in this type of meditation enhances our ability to reside in the state of self-consciousness in the midst of life.

We have learned that there are impediments to residing in the state of self-consciousness. In general, these obstacles are the various categories of identification: identification with fears and identification with desires in all their multitudinous forms. The additional requirement to properly engage in meditation is the making of ongoing efforts aimed at cleaning out psychological identifications so that quietude leading to serenity is attainable during our meditation.

e. Quieting the mind

The first purpose in meditation is to still the mind. "The mind is the great slayer of the real," Madame Blavatsky rightly says in *The Voice of the Silence*.[21] She is speaking of the lower intellectual center and lower emotional center or ordinary mind, the chattering machine that goes on in us all day long, throwing up one thought after another, one fear or desire after another, in endless succession. We each need to discover that it is so, and the practical Gurdjieff Work shows us this. Although we may not exactly understand the fourth state of consciousness that we seek to enter, we discover that whatever else is possible, it cannot happen so long as our attention is taken by the chattering mind. Therefore, all meditation techniques seek as their first purpose to quiet the mind, and there is no one method that can be claimed to be better than another. For each of us, one or another of the tried and tested techniques may work best.

Any of the following methods may be useful to still the mind. The first two methods are particularly Gurdjieffian as they involve the use of bodily sensation.

1. By including the sensation of part or all of the physical body in the attention. This is the primary method used in Gurdjieff groups. It will be explained here in detail.

2. By including the sensation of breath in the attention. This is a widely used technique and is part of the Gurdjieffian body sensing method.

3. By directly controlling thoughts. A few people are able to control thought directly.

4. By watching thoughts detachedly until the entire thought process quiets down.

5. By tracing thoughts backward, seeing how each thought has arisen from a previous thought all the way back to their source. Arriving at the source thought, it can then more easily be let go.

6. By tracing the thoughts backward with the question, who is inquiring? This technique moves the attention away from the thoughts and toward the inquirer.

7. By forcing the mind to stick to a mantra, repeated silently, not aloud. Mantra drowns out thought, but eventually the mantra also must be stopped.

8. By noticing the repetition of thoughts. This method moves the attention away from the thoughts and toward the noticer.

These methods will also serve to relax the body, and this is important because relaxation helps us to become relatively detached from the body and to conserve energy, essential ingredients for the meditative state. The first method, which is the primary Gurdjieffian method, that of including the sensation of the body in the attention, is similar to the aforementioned *nidra yoga* meditation in Hindu practice, and *vipassana* meditation in Buddhist practice. It is an exercise that has been used by many students of Gurdjieff's teaching. It seeks to expand the attention by dividing it, while relaxing bodily tension to conserve energy.

P. D. Ouspensky described this division of attention. It is recounted in lesson 2 of this book. We can also understand the exercise as the inclusion of more and more in the attention. When we attempt this, we discover that the attention is of a dynamic quality that allows its infinite expansion through intentional effort. As we intentionally include more and more in our attention, in this case more and more of the experience of our physical presence through sensation, we discover that the observer in us becomes increasingly stronger or "crystallized." Eventually, that part becomes further and further detached from identification with our personality and leads toward the greater reality of the unitive experience. As our experience of observation deepens, we come to realize that there is no observer, there is only observation.

The following account, written in the first person, describes the experience of a practitioner of this method as he engages in it each morning. You may wish to follow this procedure, varying it to accommodate to your particular situation.

f. Preparing myself for meditation (sitting)

It is early morning and still dark outside. I have intentionally awakened more than an hour before my day's activities will begin. I need this time for myself, for a different experience of my life, for another possibility about which I understand little. I relieve myself, drink a little water, and do whatever else is necessary before I go to my accustomed place for meditation.

I go to my special place, the place where I meditate. I have a place within a room that is used for other activities during the day. But now, at this early hour, I am the only one in this room. I check to see if there is adequate ventilation and if the room is at a comfortable temperature. I may need a blanket over my shoulders, and whatever else is helpful so that my sitting will be unimpaired. There is a pillow on which I regularly sit. I position it to my liking and sit down upon it. I make certain that my sitting position is comfortable and that the sphincter muscle at my rectum is comfortably closed. I make certain that the clothes I am wearing are loose so that they will not bind or otherwise discomfort me during the meditation. If needed, I sit against a wall in order to support my back. I may use an additional cushion or pillow between my back and the wall. I do these things to provide some reasonable comfort for my body so that it will more easily accommodate the demand that I shall now make upon it.

I cross my legs and place my hands one in the other in my lap. Now I am ready to begin to meditate.

I slowly and with intention close my eyes. I notice immediately that the majority of outside impressions are cut off. I also notice that sounds still enter my organism through the ears and that other outside impressions such as smells, the texture of the atmosphere, and the sensation of heat or cold, also enter and attract my attention. While these impressions may initially attract my attention, I discover that by using the body-sensing exercise described below, I am able to let go of them, and they continue mostly unnoticed in the background.

I make a tacit agreement with my body that having already ministered to its needs, I will minister to any of its further needs and wants at the end of this meditation period. But for the next period of time, be it 15 minutes or an hour, these things, itches, irritations, urinary pressure, flatulence, thirst, etc., will be held in abeyance.

I take a moment to reflect on why I am doing all this. I may have had a taste of the "something else" through previous meditation, but more likely I have not. So what I have is a theory: something I've read in a book, something that someone has told me, something that I intuit. This something has to do with another possibility for humanity in general and for each human being in particular. This something, which I confess I really do not understand although I have my opinions, is about another reality. In Gurdjieff's terms it is about the fourth and highest state of human consciousness, that which he called objective consciousness. Gurdjieff said that this state could be entered into, other than by happenstance, only through the already intentional existence in the third state of human consciousness: self-consciousness. So, I shall try through this meditative exercise to exist more deeply in the state of self-consciousness, and from that maybe something more will happen. I cannot make anything happen and I must avoid expectations, but I can put myself into the recommended conditions where something more is possible, and this is what I now attempt.

g. Describing the global body-sensing exercise

The following is a description of the global body sensing exercise. The aim is to obtain a more complete experience of oneself through a gradually more complete sensation of the physical body included in the attention. It is an exercise in expanding the attention, but what is specified here is not fixed and rigid. There is nothing unique about the bodily parts that are mentioned, nor the order in which they are included in the attention. We may want to experiment, including more or less detail as we proceed to increase the awareness of our physical presence. It is at the same time an exercise in the relaxation of muscular tension to conserve energy.

One of the things we shall almost certainly notice is that while proceeding through this exercise we "disappear." Our attention is taken by one turning thought or another, and it is only seconds or even minutes later that we realize we have not completed the establishment of a global awareness of our physical presence. In this event, it is sometimes better to just recapitulate the whole exercise, but we may discover that we need not go through it in as much detail up to the point where we "disappeared."

I begin this exercise by sensing the very top of my head, not thinking about it, but actually making the effort to have a sensation of it. Although a thought is required at the outset, the actual experience is one of physical sensation. As I go through the subsequent steps, I try to include each new sensation in the expanding attention, holding them in the attention.

I next include the sensation of my forehead with special notice to its center. This is the location of the "third eye." In *The Secret Doctrine*, earlier humanity is described as having a functioning third eye, the eye of intuition.[22] For most of us as we are now, it is only vestigial in the pineal gland, but careful observation of this area reveals a vibratory sensation that we are able to include in the attention. At the same time I recognize that thoughts, such as speculation on something like the "third eye" while in the midst of the exercise, are a diversion of the attention into identification with the thought. So, I simply lay the thought aside and continue the sensing.

I then include the sensation of the back of my head. At this point I have a more complete experience of my upper head.

I now move my attention to my eyebrows and then to my eye sockets. I sense my eyes in their sockets. I may wish to move them to the left, to the right, up, down, center, behind the closed lids. This helps me to be more aware of my eyes. I sense my eyelids as they touch each other. I inhale deeply through my nostrils several times, noticing the sensation of the inhalation of air into my organism and its subsequent exhalation. I do not interfere with the breathing. I simply observe and sense it.

I sense my ears on each side of my head, and I see that it is possible to have a sensation of them, sensing even each earlobe in addition to the upper ear.

I sense my cheeks. I may notice muscular tensions here in the small muscles of the face or, indeed, at many other places in the body as I proceed with the exercise. Wherever I encounter muscular tension, I simply, as best I can, intentionally relax those muscles. Relaxation of muscles as I proceed is a critical part of this exercise, because tensed muscles use up energy, energy which I wish to contain. My body must be relaxed if I am to transcend it. (Note: Many people find it easier to relax muscles after first tensing them as hard as they can.)

I notice the various parts of the mouth and include them in my attention: the sensation of my lips touching together, my tongue touching against my teeth and/or my palate, the moisture of the saliva in my mouth.

I sense my chin and jawbone. Here again, I may especially notice muscular tension, and if so, I simply try intentionally to relax those muscles.

At this point I realize that I have a more complete experience of my entire head. It has shape and it has weight as it rests on my neck, and I notice these things also.

I continue down the body, sensing my neck, especially its center front where I may also notice a slight vibration. This is the so-called throat *chakra*, described in the Hindu *chakra* system as one of the seven energy centers of the body, just as is the third-eye energy center mentioned already. The vibrations of energy are real and although I may notice them, I try not to go off into identification with thoughts about *chakras* or energy centers. I simply observe, sensing whatever there is to be sensed.

I sense the connection of the neck to the torso, again noticing the entire weight of the head and neck resting on the torso.

I continue further, down the left side of the body, including more and more in my attention. I could just as well have chosen to go down the right side of the body first.

I may especially notice muscular tension in the shoulders and upper back, and I simply try to relax those muscles. I sense my left shoulder, upper arm, elbow, forearm, wrist, and left hand with all its parts. I sense my thumb, forefinger, middle finger, fourth finger, little finger. I may notice moisture in the palm of my hand and the sensation of one hand touching the other.

I sense my left buttock as I pass my attention farther down the left side of the body. I notice the weight of my body on it and perhaps the texture of the cushion below it. I sense my left thigh, knee, calf, ankle, top of the left foot, heel, instep, arch, ball of the left foot, and each of the toes in order, from the big toe to the little toe, as I pass my attention down the left side of my body.

At this point it is clear to me that I have a considerably more inclusive experience of my head, neck and left side of my body than of the right side. I can verify this through my experience.

Now I circle up the right side of the body sensing each toe of the right foot in order, from the little toe to the big toe, then the top of the right foot, the ball of the foot, arch, instep, heel, ankle, calf, knee, thigh, and buttock.

I continue up the right hand, sensing the little finger, fourth finger, middle finger, forefinger, and thumb. Then I sense the palm of the hand, back of the hand, wrist, fore-arm, elbow, upper arm, and right shoulder. If I have been sitting with my hands together, I notice again the sensation of the one hand touching the other.

I continue to check for muscular tensions and when I notice them, I try intentionally to relax those muscles.

There is, at this time, a more complete global experience of myself. However, I wish also to more fully include the torso in this experience, so I intentionally breathe deeply, again noticing the inhalation and exhalation, and especially experiencing the movement of the diaphragm as my chest expands and contracts. I sense the air as it passes through my nostrils and into my lungs as I inhale and exhale. If I am a person who has learned to breathe abdominally, I also sense the movement within my abdomen as it contracts and expands.

I pass my attention down the torso from upper to lower, continuing to include more and more in the attention, sensing the solar plexus, the lower abdomen, the genitalia. I may then also wish to pass my attention from lower to upper, paralleling the spine and sensing each part of the torso in the reverse direction. I may notice a flow of vibratory energy coursing through the body rising from the area of the genitalia. I may possibly notice an additional flow of energy that seems to descend through the body from the head. Whatever I notice I simply include in my attention. All the while I am still holding the global experience of my physical presence including all my limbs, in my attention. (Students of *hatha yoga* may recognize the vibratory flow as the awakening of *kundalini*, the vibratory force usually paralleling the spine. Sometimes this is called *kundalini yoga*. Students of *tao* may understand what appears as a circular vibratory movement as the so-called "microcosmic orbit.')

Now, here I am in this place, in this moment, relaxed with this more complete experience of myself. Included in my attention is the global sensation of my physical presence, the awareness of certain external impressions that continue to come in to the attention, the experience of vibratory energy, and even thoughts and emotions that I watch detachedly. I am here now! I hold still in this state of expanded and pure attention, mind quieted, and constructively imagined or actually experienced energy coursing through the body. I am in this state and aware of being aware of myself. I am self-conscious with not even a fleeting thought in my attention.

h. Holding still in preparation for the unitive vision (objective consciousness)

Physical discomfort often sets a limit to the period of undisturbed meditation. We may, therefore, have to learn to change our position occasionally (not fidgeting) without disturbing the state of mind. This, incidentally, is one of the side benefits of getting accustomed to physical work, with all the aches and pains that must be tolerated and lived with. Thus, we learn to put up with a fair degree of discomfort before feeling forced to move. When the mind truly withdraws, the body and its discomforts are forgotten.

Another obstacle to long meditation, is the sheer habit of sleeping a fixed number of hours, with the accompanying belief that we must have our full sleep in order to be bright and alert in the competitive world. The actual need of sleep for an individual on the Fourth Way is about 4–5 hours,[23] with possibly an odd 10 minutes (or longer if possible) of withdrawal into meditation occasionally during the day, in addition to the morning meditation period. Recent medical studies insist that most human beings do not get enough sleep. Many practitioners of the Work find the opposite to be true. The point is that the state of true meditation is as restful as sleep and often more so. What we are really fighting is not the body's demands for rest, but the fixed mental belief that those demands must be satisfied. Supporting that "belief" is the conscious or subconscious knowledge that sleep is an escape. Meditation is not an escape.

Meditation exercises such as this can temporarily still the mind, but we remain, as it were, in the midst of a stilled mental process that can and does start again at any moment. Adequate stillness usually requires a period of prolonged sitting.

If we hold quiet, the next thing to look for is a slight dissociation from the thinking process, which makes it relatively easy to stay in this quiet state. It is peaceful but eventually unsatisfying. This state can deepen into the state where the body passes into sleep and we are awake within it. Deliberately invoking sleep, while keeping in a position that discourages sleep, is an aid in this process. It also points to the fact that this movement is not, initially, anything that we can achieve by intention. In practice, we have to hold in the quiet state and let ourselves get tired.

After sitting quietly for a sufficiently long period, there will occur a "shift" from the intense awareness of the body, to a total detachment from it. Here we begin to "back out," using the attention to move further and further back in our awareness from the detached body.

At this moment, through the above suggested techniques or something similar, the chain of thought will have exhausted itself, and a kind of vacuity exists before the next chain of thought begins. In this critical moment, an emotional yearning (not a thought) for self-transcendence may be set up. This moment in between chains of thought does not seem to be in time, even though it is measurable in time, because the potential experience is of a different order. This has an emotional component but it is without thought. To pass beyond into the unitive vision requires:

1. Prolonged effort.

2. Aspiration.

3. The help of maximized energy garnered through transmutation and conservation.

4.   Grace, or what appears as grace, because we have no direct control over it. Persistent perseverance without actual expectation of this "grace," which sometimes is called "help from above," is a sort of indirect control.

This effort is like leaning with our back to a door. We hold steady, steady! Eventually, the door will open of its own accord and we'll "fall" through. It is a falling through the "barrier" to the real world, free of all fear and desire. There will be a moment of unconsciousness, but then one becomes conscious in a different state. It is like falling to sleep except that in falling to sleep you just go unconscious and stay that way. Here, after the moment of unconsciousness, one is conscious of standing in the bigger self, of seeing things from a more detached perspective, the perspective of the unitive vision. Passing through the "barrier" can be an ecstatic experience, but it does not necessarily happen to all people as some sort of dramatic thing. Some people do just ease into it.

i. The unitive vision

The unitive experience or unitive vision is the ultimate objective of meditation. But the different terms used to describe it: the "real world," "objective consciousness," "enlightenment," all lack specificity in helping us to understand just what it is. It has been said that the unitive experience cannot be described in words, although numerous people have attempted a description. Thomas Merton, the Christian mystic, was one of many people who have tried to describe the ecstasy of his awakening into the unitive vision. His description of it is representative:

> We enter a region which we had never even suspected, and yet it is this new world which seems familiar and obvious. The old world of our senses is now the one that seems to us strange, remote and unbelievable ...

> A door opens in the center of our being and we seem to fall through it into immense depths which, although they are infinite, are all accessible to us; all eternity seems to have become ours in this one placid and breathless contact ...

> You seem to be the same person and you are the same person that you have always been: in fact you are more yourself than you have ever been before.

> You have only just begun to exist. You feel as if you were at last fully born. All that went before was a mistake, a fumbling preparation for birth. Now you have come out into your element. And yet now you have become nothing. You have sunk to the center of your own poverty, and there you have felt the doors fly open into infinite freedom, into a wealth which is perfect because none of it is yours and yet it all belongs to you. And now you are free to go in and out of infinity ...

> And you, while you are free to come and go, yet as soon as you attempt to make words or thoughts about it you are excluded – you go back into your exterior in order to talk. [24]

The "breathless contact" written of by Merton is that which takes place in the vacuity between two chains of thought. The region he describes is not in the world of the senses and, therefore, does not seem to the meditator to be experienced in passing time.

Once we have had the experience of breaking through, we will know that the experience has been had. It will then not necessarily be repeatable at will, but the direction in which to go will be known, and continuing efforts will eventually bring about repeated access. Having had the experience, we will want to watch, observe, stick at it, even push. We are bound to make "mistakes," but we cannot find the right track without trying out a few wrong ones.

We need to remember, if we get stuck with nothing happening, it is likely to be because we think we ourself can do it, the ordinary mundane "I," whereas that "I" can only serve the higher being that does the thing. Therefore, we may have to go on sitting and watching for longer than we need to at first. We cannot make something happen. We simply make ourselves available for the experience.

This step of "passing beyond" is that for which earlier work should prepare us for un-termed periods of sitting. Although we may be able to arrive at a sufficient quietude after about 20 minutes of sitting, we need to allow sufficient time after that, during which we make ourselves available to further experience. It is best not to set up a predetermined time limit.

It must be remembered that the sort of instruction being given here is for people who have practiced long enough to have formed a degree of self-consciousness through the preliminary exercises. Only then is there something to stay awake when the barrier is passed.

It is best if the thing that we are seeking can be understood in more subtle terms, so that the attention can be turned in the right direction, and some sort of "active imagination" can be put to practical use. But for this to work, there has to be full acceptance of the reality of subtle energies. "Active imagination" cannot work if it is thought to be mere imagination.

Once we have learned to transcend the barrier, teaching of a higher order can be received. This does not necessarily mean that there will be visions of a wise sage propounding great wisdom. Often, teaching is received simply as insight that appears to come from, we know not where, from the very center of our being. At the same time, images received in the deep meditative state, as distinguished from turning thoughts or imaginative reveries, should be carefully noted for the purpose of familiarization, before they are set aside.

We should realize that facility in meditative practice is ordinarily attainable only with long experience. So we need not be discouraged at any apparent lack of success, and we must remember that our work is to provide the conditions for a different experience, not to presume that we can generate the experience itself.

j. An exercise in consciousness: meditation
Meditation must be practiced every day at least once each day, preferably upon arising. It is a daily reminder to function in self-consciousness as we proceed through our day. Its quietude provides us the best conditions to experience the dividing of attention. Dividing of the attention is necessary to commence the separation of the real self from the personality. Remember Gurdjieff's dictum: "As long as a man (or woman) does not separate himself from himself he can achieve nothing and no one can help him." During this next week, let us take it as an exercise that every day we will go somewhere in our home and sit quietly using the meditative techniques that have been suggested here or something similar. It is important that this morning sitting become a primary and regular part of our day, something that we will not want to skip.

> Meditation may be the one essential practice, without which nothing of significance will happen. [25]

But we need to caution ourselves that more is required of us than just sitting in silence once or twice each day.

> The requirements of total self-dedication cannot be met by an hour or two's practice. One cannot be totally "given" at some times of the day and following one's own self-ish interests at other times. The attempt has to be made to bring the totality of one's nature into harmony with one's perceptions of the nature and source of being. [26]

Lesson 6

Gurdjieff groups

For where two or three come together in my name, there I am with them.
(Matthew, 18:19–21)

a. Am I able to meditate?

Let us examine and share our experiences with respect to meditation. Was I able to sit quietly each day since the exercise to meditate was given? What technique did I use? For how long did I sit? At what time of the day? What did I observe about forces that prevented me from sitting regularly? Observations about our effort to meditate are especially useful in showing us the extent of our will.

Even if we do not yet understand the importance of daily meditation, we should take it as an exercise that we shall attempt each day. However difficult we find this exercise, we must decide to attempt it every day. We must intentionally give over a portion of each day to a different experience of ourselves, to engagement with our inner life. And we must make this effort primary, giving it value and putting it ahead of all external activities. Frankly speaking, it is unlikely that any change will occur in us if we do not accustom ourselves to sitting quietly for a time at least once each day.

Now, for the remainder of this sixth lesson, let us take it as an exercise to sit with both feet on the floor. Notice while examining this material how often we revert or attempt to revert to the habitual posture of sitting with our legs crossed. Going against habitual postures helps us to be conscious of ourselves. We need to resolve to always go against such habits and certainly when we meet as a group.

b. The importance of a group

The passage from *The New Testament* at the head of this lesson suggests, as do many other passages in *The Bible*, a meaning that is hidden and yet is in plain view. It speaks of the necessity of meeting with others because in meeting with others, "there 'I' am." We take "I" to mean Jesus in the above passage, but in Gurdjieff's terms "I" is permanent "I." It is that state in which I know that I am Endlessness.

Gurdjieff viewed Jesus as one of several great historical figures, including the Buddha, who were enlightened beings. By this he meant that such a being knows that there is no distinction between him or herself and that state which Gurdjieff calls "Endlessness." It is in this sense that Jesus is "God" and so are we all. The only difference is that Jesus knew who he was, but we, identified with our personality, do not yet know who we are.

It is our task, through the Work, to discover who we are. In that discovery we find that there is no one: no priest, no minister, no rabbi, no imam, no Gurdjieff group leader, who is delegated to stand between us and our true nature, that nature which Gurdjieff also calls permanent "I." It is that state in which we are present to ourselves, that condition in which we are self-conscious and that condition in which we are conscious of who we are. We can verify that we are rarely in that state without making intentional effort. Having attempted the self-consciousness exercises that have been suggested, we know how difficult it is to remember ourselves. We are completely identified with our personality, that tissue of sensations and memories that we mistakenly call "I." This leaves no room in our attention for the experience of ourselves.

Much of the time we will have entirely forgotten the exercise to remember ourselves. This is to be expected because such as we are, we have no real will. But when we commit ourselves to meet with others, to meet as a group, it is the group itself that provides the will that helps us to be self-conscious until we are sufficiently conscious to have developed real will.

There are exceptions to the need for a group. We have heard or read of great beings who have done the Work on themselves in a solitary fashion. The great Indian saint Ramana Maharshi was known to have had a profound experience of enlightenment at the age of 17 years. After that experience, he was content to live in the courtyard of a temple in south India. With others or alone, it made no difference.

But for the great majority of us, having verified our inability to remain self-conscious for more than a moment, we discover that we need others to remind us and to make a demand upon us to work on ourselves. The group meeting, usually weekly, at which we discuss our observations of ourselves, makes this demand.

There are other benefits of people meeting together as a group. There is, for example, the social interaction that we enjoy, the camaraderie, and the effort of a group that helps to get things done, whether tending a garden or building a house. There is the benefit of friction if we work with others in a group, "rubbing up" against others in working on some task. In doing so, we can observe ourselves and our reactions to what we take to be the unpleasant manifestation of others. But it is the group will, substituting temporarily for our own lack of will to be self-conscious, that is the primary value of a group of people meeting together.

c. Existing groups and payment

Gurdjieff groups have been organized along various lines and serve their members in a variety of ways. If we are able to find an existing group within which we can take a part, we are fortunate, because the organizational work of setting up such a group has already been done. Such a group will likely be led or facilitated by an older student(s) who has previous experience in the Work and who presumably understands more than we who are newer to these ideas.

Gurdjieff spoke about the necessity for a student on the way to put another person in his or her place in order for that student to go further. As a practical matter, it should be obvious that if an older student cannot explain to a newer student what he or she understands about the Work, then there is a very real question about the level of that person's understanding. In addition, the existence of a group that has been organized by an older student places a greater demand upon that student to be self-conscious than is the demand placed upon newer students. For these reasons, group work is even more important for the person who leads or facilitates a group than it is for the group members, although the value of group work is important for all and cannot be overestimated.

Among external activities often undertaken by Gurdjieff groups are, for example, cooking, gardening, working with crafts, and so forth. These kinds of activities meet the social needs of the members along with generating friction amongst them to help them to observe themselves. All these activities can be supportive of the primary purpose of the group, which is always to provide a kind of temporary will in substitution for the inadequate will of group members to make the continuing effort necessary to be self-conscious.

Gurdjieff said that there were three lines of work. First, there is work on oneself, by which we study the ideas, and engage in all manner of exercises in the effort to be self-conscious. Second, there is work with others, which is facilitated by participating in a group. The work with others, in addition to sharing our observations in relation to a weekly group exercise, supports the effort of each of us to be self-conscious, and helps us to observe our negative identifications as we "rub" up against others, enduring their unpleasant manifestations. Third, there is work for the Work. This has to do with organizing and maintaining the Work through groups and other activities so that the Work remains alive and can be found by others. The more of these three lines of work that we engage in, the greater the demand for consciousness that is put upon us and the less is the waking sleep in which we are enthralled.

Unfortunately, there are people who, knowing something about the teaching, organize groups for their own ego aggrandizement and/or for the power and money that such a group may bring to them. Gurdjieff called such people rogues and charlatans. In looking for a group, be careful! Use your good common sense and beware of any extraordinary demands for money. A demand, for example, that you pay to the group or its leader a percentage of your income or other such inappropriate financial scheme is a tip-off that you may be about to get fleeced.

There is a tradition in many esoteric groups that the older student or leader must not be supported by the younger students. The leader must have his or her own source of livelihood. This is an additional protection from a false leader who uses a group as a source for his/her own material wealth. Gurdjieff was his own best example of this tradition in the many ventures in which he engaged for his own livelihood. He sold carpets, he sold corsets, he sold false eyelashes, and he engaged in numerous other business enterprises during his life. While there may be some circumstances in which there are really good reasons for younger students to support the older student/leader, a cautionary note is sounded when a group functions in material support of the leader.

Some fees are necessary, as they would be in any group, not just a Gurdjieff group. Supplies need to be purchased, a facility needs to be rented, and so on. But these kinds of expenses are reasonable and not onerous, especially when divided over a number of people. Perhaps the first test of suitability for anyone approaching the Gurdjieff Work is their ability to use good common sense and to not get fleeced.

d. Organizing a group

If a legitimate existing Gurdjieff group is not available to us, we can organize a group ourselves. This is no easy task and it is really better for the newer student to learn first-hand and orally from "one who knows" what this Work is about. But when this is not possible, the effort to organize a group will serve the student well. However, it would be presumptuous and almost certainly personality-enhancing to organize such a group setting oneself up as its leader. This is exactly opposite to the work of making the personality passive that is an essential part of the teaching. So, great care must be taken. A person attempting to organize such work should see him or herself as a facilitator and fellow student rather than as a leader or teacher.

Through engaging in 1) the study of *Beelzebub's Tales to His Grandson*, along with the other two primary pillars of the work, 2) group exercises leading toward self-consciousness, especially as suggested in the pages of *Beelzebub's Tales to His Grandson*, and 3) daily meditation, the student really cannot go wrong. In fact, the person who undertakes to organize such work benefits the most because of additional demands for self-consciousness made upon that person. By making the organizational effort required to establish a group, we are helped to remember ourselves, and the group will similarly help whoever else joins us in this Work. Gurdjieff has given us all the tools we need through *Beelzebub's Tales to His Grandson*. In it, he said, are all the keys, only they are not near their locks. So, it becomes our job to find those keys and the locks into which they fit. Gurdjieff predicted that in future years, the book will be read from pulpits all over the world. We who know of the book are able to use it now.

Remember that even two or three constitute a group, and if a group gets too large it becomes ineffective, because there is insufficient time at the weekly meeting for everyone to speak about their observations during the week. For this reason, large Gurdjieff groups that have come about over the years have needed to subdivide themselves for the purpose of a group meeting.

There is no reward for large numbers. In fact, if we go after numbers we will lose our way. This is because the motive of personal aggrandizement enters into the effort, and enhancement of the personality is exactly opposite of enlightenment. In enlightenment we know that we are one and that there is no separation between any of us.

So, what does a group do? Since Gurdjieff's death, groups of all kinds have sprung up in pursuit of the teaching. Gurdjieff brought us a feast of ideas and methods. Groups use a wide variety of techniques. Some techniques can be shown to have been used by Gurdjieff while he himself taught, but others seem to be the invention of those who have led a particular group. It is maintained here that at least three primary elements are necessary for useful group work:

1.   A group must meet regularly, preferably weekly.

2.   A group reads and discusses together *Beelzebub's Tales to His Grandson*.

3.   A group encourages its members to meditate.

However, a group may also engage in many other activities, in particular the second line of work, working with others, and engaging as a group in the Gurdjieff Movements. These last two activities are usually undertaken by members of a large established group and generally require the use of an appropriate physical property. But a group of any size, however small, may engage in useful work by engaging in the three primary elements.

These three primary elements of group work can be undertaken by a group of as few as two or three, as outlined below.

1. Weekly meetings

A group must meet regularly and often, because the members use the meeting to make a demand upon themselves to use the tool of attention for the experience of self-consciousness. The individuals in such a group have further agreed to undertake striving exercises, reminding exercises, and self-observation exercises in their ordinary life in pursuit of self-consciousness. The group meetings are used by the members to recount their observations and experiences vis-à-vis these weekly exercises. This is the principal demand of the Fourth Way, and the existence of the group by its nature makes this demand for self-consciousness upon its members, a demand which each member by him or herself may not be capable of making.

2. The recommended text

If, as has been hypothesized here, Gurdjieff wrote *Beelzebub's Tales to His Grandson* in a particular way, so that it will have a particular effect on the reader–listener, then we, as his students, just as Hassein, as Beelzebub's student in the story, will begin to be changed by the reading of this book. Note that at the beginning of the book, Gurdjieff recommends that it be read not once, but three times. The first time, he suggests, the book should be read as we are already accustomed to read, that is in our ordinary mechanical way. The second time it should be read as if we were reading aloud to another person, and the third time while trying to fathom the gist of his writings.

The suggestion for the second reading, as if we were reading aloud to another person, should be taken literally. What we receive through our aural faculty has the ability to bypass the intellect and to fall directly on our emotions. This is especially important because the emotional center is much quicker and more powerful than the intellectual center. Gurdjieff pointed out that the speeds at which the three lower centers work differ vastly from each other. The speed of the intellectual center is much slower than the speed of the moving/instinctive center, and the speed of the moving/instinctive center, in turn, is much slower than the speed of the emotional center. By having ideas fall directly on the emotions through hearing them, they are imbibed and processed with great rapidity and force.

Then there are the vibrations caused within our organism when we hear the special sounds that are generated by the vocabulary of more than 500 unique words that Gurdjieff uses. Whether these special sounds have an esoterically salutary effect upon the hearer is something subject to each person's personal verification.

The hundreds of objectively impartial criticisms of the life of man scattered throughout *Beelzebub's Tales to His Grandson* have a cumulative effect upon the psyche of the reader or listener. Through these criticisms, we discover how our improper education from the time of our birth has caused us to lose our sense of purpose. Through these criticisms we begin to realize how foolish has been much of human behavior through the centuries. Through the impact of these criticisms on us, the process of change, which Gurdjieff has termed *metanoia*, begins. Gurdjieff has told us of this, having expressed it by declaring his stated purpose in writing *Beelzebub's Tales to His Grandson*:

> To destroy, mercilessly, without any compromises whatsoever, in the mentation and feelings of the reader, the beliefs and views, by centuries rooted in him, about everything existing in the world. [27]

If a group is facilitated by a student who is completely unfamiliar with *Beelzebub's Tales to His Grandson*, that student may decide to adopt initially one of the other well known texts of the Work to serve for talking points and for the generation of exercises. Ouspensky's *In Search of the Miraculous* and Nicoll's *Psychological Commentaries on the Teaching of Gurdjieff and Ouspensky*, among other texts, have been commonly used. These can serve usefully as starting points of the Gurdjieff literature, but eventually the group and its facilitator will want to undertake the more difficult *Beelzebub's Tales to His Grandson* for its profound benefit.

3. Meditation

Meditation is a solitary effort, but through the group, meditative instruction can be given, and meditative instruction is most effective when given orally and through demonstration. Without meditation, it is unlikely that any real change will occur in the student. A periodic group meditation is supportive of the solitary meditational effort to be made by the student each day.

Typically, a group meeting is held weekly and, depending upon the number of members, will last for between 1 and 2 hours. This provides adequate time, first for each group member to speak about his or her self-observations during the week, addressing the agreed upon exercise, and second, to read and discuss a portion of *Beelzebub's Tales to His Grandson*. Within its pages, Gurdjieff suggests all manner of exercises. Appendix 3 gives a listing of key words suggesting group exercises to promote self-consciousness. Some exercises are based upon what Gurdjieff has suggested, while others are based on the suggestions of students. This list need not be taken rigidly, and groups continually invent new exercises in furtherance of self-consciousness.

e. The three categories of practical exercises

The exercises generally undertaken by people engaged in practical Gurdjieff Work can be divided into three categories. These are distinct from the specialized exercises that are not taken up in this text but are also given as part of the teaching, such as those related to sacred dance (the Gurdjieff Movements) or memorization exercises.

The first category of exercises can be seen as principal exercises or, to use Gurdjieff's term, "strivings." Unlike the second and third categories of exercises, which need to be changed from week to week, these are to be practiced always and everywhere. We need to remember to engage in them. They help to shake us loose from the erroneous idea that we are the personality and from our identification with it. Practiced over a long period of time, these exercises or strivings free us from this erroneous identification and we come to realize that the personality (our body, emotions and thoughts) is only a tool. It is the vehicle, physical, emotional, and mental, through which we manifest as human beings for the experience of self-consciousness. We encountered one of these principal exercises in attempting to put ourselves in the position of another person.

The second category of exercises refers to those that remind us to be aware of being aware of ourselves. They can be called reminding or "stop" exercises, because they require us to stop, to sense ourselves, and to be aware of being aware of ourselves in the moment. We encountered this category of exercise in the exercise of making a stop before commencing each meal, and in the exercise of stopping in the doorway of our home as we go in and out. While not a "stop" in the technical sense that requires a person outside of us to call "stop," these reminders help us to be self-conscious.

The third category of exercises comprises psychological exercises in which we observe a particular feature of identification in ourselves, usually a type of so-called negative emotion. These psychological features take our attention and our energy, the very energy that is needed to stand in objective consciousness. The exercise of the self-observation of internal considering in which we have already engaged is a typical example.

f. Principal exercises or strivings

Overriding the many exercises created by Gurdjieff himself and numerous students of Gurdjieff's teaching to be undertaken from time to time, there are what we can call "principal exercises or strivings." Unlike exercises which must be changed from time to time because they become mechanical, these are exercises which we need to strive to engage in always and everywhere. They are specifically given by Gurdjieff in *Beelzebub's Tales to His Grandson*. Such as we are, we cannot successfully engage in these exercises on a continuing basis, but they can be seen as exercises toward which we strive to engage in always and everywhere. The first five are enumerated as the being-obligolnian strivings (see page 386 of *Beelzebub's Tales to His Grandson*). The exact wording is given in lesson 3 (page 30) of this book. In contemporary language they are:

1.   To strive to have everything satisfying and really necessary for our planetary body.

2.   To strive constantly for self-perfection in the sense of being.

3.	To strive to know ever more concerning the laws of world-creation and world-maintenance. [These are the laws governing the structure of ourselves (the microcosm) and the larger universe of which we are a reflection (the macrocosm). These two great laws are also known as the law of the three forces (the sacred triamazikamno) and the law of the octave (the sacred heptaparaparshinokh).]

4.	To strive to pay for our arising and individuality as quickly as possible. [We need to consider what this really means. There are many ways to pay.]

5.	To strive to assist the most rapid perfecting of other beings, both those similar to ourselves and those of other forms.

In addition to these five being-obligolnian strivings, seven more principal exercises or strivings are also given in *Beelzebub's Tales to His Grandson* and in the third series of Gurdjieff's writings, *Life is real only then, when "I am."* These additional exercises are:

6.	To strive to watch the reflection of the splendor of the sunrise every day in the state of self-consciousness. Its significance becomes clear when we do this because we realize that it is a daily reminder of relativity. It puts earth and all the events upon it in perspective as less than the significance of a grain of sand in the universal plan. (See page 78 of *Beelzebub's Tales to His Grandson.*) In practice, since the Fourth Way is a way in the midst of life, a student, for reasons of work in life or something similar, who cannot be available to watch the sunrise, can select another cosmic event during the course of each day. For example, we can watch the sunset or moonrise or moonset or the starry sky.

7.	To strive to meditate each day. (See page 355 of *Beelzebub's Tales to His Grandson.*)

8.	To strive to consciously labor. In all our activities we must always strive to act or labor consciously in the sense of Gurdjieff's meaning of human consciousness. These are the third and fourth states of consciousness. The third state is self-consciousness in which we include ourselves in our attention. The fourth state is objective consciousness in which the identity of the individual with the universal is perceived. (See page 792 of *Beelzebub's Tales to His Grandson.*)

9.	To strive to intentionally suffer. (See page 792 of *Beelzebub's Tales to His Grandson.*) Gurdjieff explains this by giving, as an example, the greatest intentional suffering. This is to compel ourselves to be able to endure the displeasing manifestations of others towards us. (See page 242 of *Beelzebub's Tales to His Grandson.*) He also simplified this striving with the aphorism, that we must like what "it" does not like, "it" referring to the personality.

10. To strive to put ourselves in the position of other beings, both those similar to ourselves and those of other forms. This is striving to put ourselves in the other person's shoes because in essence we are the other person. In essence we are all other beings. (See page 1164 of *Beelzebub's Tales to His Grandson*.)

11. To strive to constantly sense and be cognizant of the inevitability of our own death as well as of the death of everyone upon whom our eyes or attention rests. (See page 1183 of *Beelzebub's Tales to His Grandson*.)

12. To strive to manifest "as if" we already stand in objective consciousness. Gurdjieff considered this a useful form of self-deception. In other traditions it is seen as constructive imagination. In theory, if a person who stands in objective consciousness experiences a certain form of manifestation, such as a vibratory reverberation in certain parts of the body or a particular world view, then by manifesting as if we experience such a vibration or such a world view, we can bring their experience into our reality because it is a real experience otherwise not noticed by us. (See *Life is real only then, when "I am,"* pages 132–136.)

g. The reminding and "stop" category of exercises

The reminding and "stop" category of exercises are those that remind us to be conscious of ourselves in the moment. Three of these, for example, have come down to us in distorted form in the customs of religious practices. Two of them have been given as exercises earlier in this text. Each of these can serve as a Gurdjieff exercise for a week or more. In theory they, like the principal exercises, should be practiced always and everywhere. In practice, they tend to become mechanical but we can strive to implement them as often as possible. Gurdjieff groups make up all manner of variations of reminding and stop exercises.

In the technical sense in which Gurdjieff used the term "stop" exercise, it requires that "stop" be invoked by a separate person. No one can call a "stop" on themselves because the element of surprise is missing. That separate person was often Gurdjieff himself in the groups that he led. He would shout "stop," for example, to a surprised group of people engaged in sacred dance. In that moment of "stop," the dancers have a profound experience of self-consciousness, self-observing their thoughts, emotions, and postures, and conscious of themselves in their attention.

For our purposes in constructing exercises of the reminder and "stop" types, the surprise comes to us in the sudden reminder that the construction of the exercise itself is designed to invoke.

The three examples of exercises given below can serve as inspiration for whatever variations any group wishes.

The first example is the making of a "stop" before commencing each meal. For most of us who eat three meals each day, this exercise will serve as a "stop" three times in the day. As always, in the moment of remembering the exercise, we come back to the experience of being aware of being aware of ourselves in our attention through sensation of the physical body. When we make this "stop" at the commencement of the meal, we then try to continue with the experience of self-consciousness for as long as possible throughout the meal. This exercise is practiced in many monasteries where the inhabitants are aware of its significance. In less spiritually demanding circumstances and often in a family setting, sitting around the breakfast or dinner table, it has taken the form of saying a prayer, the saying of grace, before commencing the meal. For those who understand the significance of "stop," this is a very powerful exercise. Even for those who are not aware of the inner significance, the "stop" of mouthing a prayer at the onset of a meal can have beneficial effects, because at least a slight amount of reminding and stop inevitably takes place.

The second example of these exercises is the making of a "stop" for some seconds while standing at the bedside just before getting into bed at night, and a similar "stop" standing at the bedside just as we arise from sleep in the morning. The saying of bedside prayers, as is a custom in many religious traditions, is a "stop" even if the person praying is not aware of the true significance.

The third of these "stop" exercises, also based upon religious tradition, is that of making a "stop" each time we go in or out the door of our house.

> The lord is one ... These words that I command you today...write them upon the door-frames of your houses and on your gates. (Deuteronomy, 6:4–9)

In the religion of Judaism, the biblical command to post these words on the door-frame of one's house is typically obeyed by installing them on the door-frame in a small container known as a *mezuzah*. As is the case with the saying of a prayer before the start of each meal and the saying of bedside prayers, the inner significance of the *mezuzah* stop is no longer widely known.

h. Psychological exercises for observing identifications

As we have seen, the self-observation of psychological states of identification that keep us from self-consciousness and that drain us of energy are a major part of the Gurdjieff Work. Many exercises to help us in self-observation have been devised by Gurdjieff and by students of the teaching. The exercise of observing internal considering that was given earlier is an example of such a psychological exercise. Appendix 3 includes another example of a psychological exercise called by Gurdjieff "wiseacring" along with keyword lists from which similar exercises can be constructed.

i. Gurdjieff music

Any introduction to Gurdjieff's teaching would be incomplete if it does not mention his music and his Movements. Gurdjieff brought his teaching in various ways to appeal to various "types" of people. He took the science of "types" as a major part of his own work. To reach various "types" of people he used what he called "objective music" and sacred temple dances (known now as the Gurdjieff Movements), along with an intellectual exposition of his teaching, readings from *Beelzebub's Tales to His Grandson* and practical work on self by way of the Fourth Way exercises. Certain types of people will never open a book, others cannot sense rhythms, still others are tone-deaf. Gurdjieff attempted to reach them all.

Our consciousness is not made up of mental concepts and ideas only; it also encompasses our feelings and our spiritual impulses. Our real feelings and emotions are mostly strongly hindered in ordinary life, much more so than we can imagine. But we can come closer to them through objective music which affects all people similarly. This must not be confused with subjective music, which affects some people one way, other people another way, and still other people not at all. It is not possible to speak as easily about real objective music as it is about ideas and thoughts. Of course, musical theory can be learned and spoken about, if one knows the appropriate vocabulary. But to speak about it, however learnedly, is not the same thing as to listen to it or rather to truly hear it. There is a great difference between simply listening, perhaps while thinking about something else, and hearing, that is, making an intentional voluntary effort to be consciously attentive to what one listens to, while at the same time including the experience of ourselves in our attention.

Gurdjieff often used music, especially in relation to the music accompanying special movements and the sacred dances he apparently had witnessed during his travels. Early on, he attempted to transmit his teaching through these methods to pupils for whom they were suited. He was able, with the help of an early pupil, the musician Thomas de Hartmann, to reproduce the sacred objective music.

Gurdjieff's music, conscious, objective music, touches our deepest impulses and liberates them from their chains, not all at once, but gradually and surely. Some of our inner knots, our complexes, our tensions, and bad habits, even the most deeply rooted ones, are also touched and freed by this special music. It is an objective, conscious, music because it has a conscious aim. Whether Gurdjieff observed and remembered the music from his travels on this earth or whether it came from a deeper and more distant place in himself remains an open question. In either case, the purpose of such music is to help us to become more conscious of ourselves. This expansion of consciousness, if we obtain it, whether through music or in any other way, is not limited to the development of our mental capacities. Objective music improves the perception of our normal bodily sensations, and of our true feelings as well as our capability to think consciously. And consciousness of feeling is connected to "conscience," which also is rarely free to manifest itself. The aim is a global expansion of consciousness.

j. Sacred dance: the Gurdjieff Movements

Gurdjieff placed great importance on sacred dance as a method of teaching. Whether Gurdjieff was allowed to see the sacred dances in Middle Eastern and oriental temples and to later study them in the (still undiscovered) supposed monastery of the "Sarmoung Brotherhood" about which he wrote, or whether he brought them from a place more distant in time and space is not known to us. Gurdjieff's interpretation of them have become known as the Gurdjieff Movements, of which there are several hundred, some being regarded as special Movements themselves and others as preliminary exercises.

The study of the Movements can be seen as a specialized kind of Gurdjieff exercise. For some Gurdjieff groups, they are the centerpiece of Gurdjieff's teaching, and participants engage in Movements classes once each week or more. A group is necessary for participation since the Movements inevitably require several participants to engage in them together. Some Gurdjieff students who have specialized in the study of the Movements offer "Movements Intensives" and workshops throughout the year in various parts of the world. Information about these can be found on the Internet.

Many Movements require the participant to engage various parts of the body simultaneously in different rhythms. At a certain point in this activity, the intellectual center gives up its control and a balance is struck between the moving/instinctive, the emotional, and the intellectual center. The participant, then in a profound state of self-consciousness, experiences in detachment the activity that is taking place.

Without actual participation, a student cannot properly appreciate the Movements, and descriptive words are generally inadequate. However, an exponent of the Gurdjieff Movements, Pauline de Dampierre, who was a student of Gurdjieff in Paris in the 1940s, attempted some explanation in an interview conducted for *The American Theosophist* in 1985. When asked how to describe them she said:

> How to describe them – perhaps there's no better way than the answer Gurdjieff gave to his pupil Ouspensky, when he told him to imagine that there was a mechanism for studying the planets which represented visually the laws governing their movements, reminding the onlooker of all he knows about the solar system. He said there was something like that in the rhythm of the sacred dances.

Of the participant's experience, she went on to say:

> The first requirement is for the correct pure position; otherwise the meaning is lost. The position becomes something less unconscious. Schematically, let's say that it's a firm, balanced position, that allows the person to maintain an inner presence while making a simple gesture, followed through without tension, without any useless or involuntary expenditure of energy. One has to feel the position, having a living impression of it, for it to be right and pure …

> Again and again, while making the movement, the pupil tries to return to himself and to remember the direction of his search. He must have a deeper, more relaxed, more sustained attention …

> But if this attention is sustained, a new energy appears which is higher and more active, which awakens him to himself. The body relaxes completely and begins to participate in a freer way; a new intelligence accompanies the movement. At the moment, the pupil approaches the "exact doing" of which Gurdjieff spoke.[28]

k. *Beelzebub's Tales to His Grandson*

Beelzebub's Tales to His Grandson, Gurdjieff's *magnum opus*, has been referred to frequently in this text. Special attention needs to be given to this work because of its extraordinary nature. With the exception of a few earlier writings, Gurdjieff intended his entire literary effort to be contained in one overall work, which he called *All and Everything*. It was to consist of 10 books in three series. The title given to the first of these three series was *An Objectively Impartial Criticism of the Life of Man or Beelzebub's Tales to his Grandson*. Although the second series was eventually put out as a quasi-autobiographical book entitled *Meetings With Remarkable Men*, and a third, apparently never completed, series was also published under the title *Life is real only then, when "I am"*, it was the first series that became the centerpiece of Gurdjieff's work during the latter part of his life from 1924 until his passing in 1949. As originally published, the first series took on the name of the overall work, *All and Everything*. In later editions it became known as *Beelzebub's Tales to His Grandson*, with the subtitle of *An Objectively Impartial Criticism of the Life of Man*.

While masquerading as a space odyssey, the supposed plot of which is described in Appendix 4, *Beelzebub's Tales to His Grandson* contains layer upon layer of subtle meaning. It works its magic on those who make the effort required to read it. There is no doubt that the hundreds of objectively impartial criticisms of the life of man given throughout the book have a profound effect on us, causing us to seriously question our behavior. Possibly even more important is the vibratory effect on our organism of hearing and pronouncing the more than 500 special words created by Gurdjieff and that appear throughout the text. In this sense, but always subject to our own personal verification about such speculation, the book is magic.

l. Toasts to the idiots

One of the more unusual activities that Gurdjieff employed in his teaching is what was known as the "Toasts to the Idiots." At ritualistic meals hosted by him, mainly in his Paris apartment in his latter years, he would sometimes ask his diners to declare what kind of idiots they were. Toasts were then drunk to them. He used the term not only pejoratively, but also in the sense of the Greek root of the word, which goes toward describing a person's type. Gurdjieff was very much interested in the various types of people and the levels of their being. He developed a list of 21 different categories of idiots, and he often told people what kinds of idiot they were. For a more detailed description of this activity, including Gurdjieff's list of categories of idiots, see James Moore's *Gurdjieff: The Anatomy of a Myth.*[29]

Since Gurdjieff's passing in 1949, students have generally discontinued this activity, most feeling inadequate to the task of assessing to which category of idiot any particular person belongs. However, individual students have sometimes taken it as an exercise to assess for themselves which type of idiot they are.

m. For whom is the Gurdjieff Work suited?

Gurdjieff used a Russian word, *obyvatel*, in describing to Ouspensky what we might call a responsible adult. This is someone who has dealt with the matters that life has placed before him or her in a responsible way. Such a person would more than likely be at least in their thirties and often a good deal older. This person would have had enough experience of life to have had the opportunities to deal with the events of life in a responsible way.

Notwithstanding their having met life's issues responsibly, a small number of such people have a gnawing feeling that there must be more to life than what they had so far perceived. They begin to ask the big questions mentioned in the first lesson: who am I and what is the purpose of human life? They then go in search of knowledge, often knowledge that is not ordinary. It is what we might call occult knowledge.

While there are exceptions, younger people, in their twenties and younger, who come to these ideas, are often looking for an escape from life's responsibilities rather than dealing with them. The Work is not an escape. Consequently, most people studying Gurdjieff's teaching tend to be in their thirties, forties, fifties, and even older.

n. How long is the duration of this Work?

The Gurdjieff Work is an essentially practical teaching. Although it contains a rich cosmology that may be studied and pondered upon, that cosmology is only the road map. Doing the work is the practical application of the techniques that Gurdjieff brought.

When people approach this teaching, they often ask how long will it take for the practice of the Work to begin to effect change in them? It is not an unreasonable question. In answer to this question, Gurdjieff pointed out to Ouspensky that generally it takes about 5 years for the basic study of medicine and perhaps twice as long to learn about music or painting. So it should not surprise us that many years of Work are required before real change begins to take place in us.

Once our eyes have been opened a little and we are less soundly asleep, we each have to give our willing consent and, in some sense, confirm our conscious self-dedication to the Work. If we refuse, we condemn ourselves to insignificance, to a series of lives that dim out in meaningless repetition. In this lifetime, as we approach old age, we are confronted with the diminishment of our significance, no matter what our worldly achievements, because of the impermanence of the personality. But through the Work, the immense value of our life experience, as reflected in personality, is integrated into the all-consuming unity of being in which we stand. Standing in the unity, we experience true freedom.

o. Love

Gurdjieff's view that genuine love is a sacred-being impulse cannot be overemphasized. A distinction must be made between genuine love and what passes for love in our society, based upon polarity or type. It is only when we are completely free of all fear and all desire, and our personal selfhood is integrated into the all-consuming unity of being, that we experience the sacred-being impulse of genuine love. In that state we know that we are Endlessness, as is everything else, and our love therefore extends to everyone and everything because they are all us. Thus, the sacred-being impulse of genuine love experienced in the unitive vision more than anything else is an objective measure of how long is the duration of this work.

> Love is the light and love is the way. Where ere love's camels turn, the one true way is there. (A favorite Sufi saying of Sri Madhava Ashish)

p. Conclusion

To sum up: we attribute to ourselves consciousness, free-will, willpower, the ability to choose what we want, and the power to do what we want, when in fact we have none of these capacities. If we do not first realize the lack of these attributes, we cannot begin to remedy the situation. However, as soon as we become aware of our lack and the realization that we manifest only as personalities, the impermanent and therefore not objectively real entities who have none of the qualities we thought we had, we begin then to perceive the obstacles standing in our way and to look for the means to overcome them.

We also search for a way that will bring us back to what we should be, that is, we set out on the quest for the "path of return" to the realization of our divine nature, the source of consciousness. If we search diligently, we find a mentor or a group. If need be, we find others and organize a group. Then we can go on our way step by step, and ultimately reach the desired destination where we will discover what we thought we already knew: who we are and what is our purpose.

For humankind's survival, our sorry state must be made known to us, so as to make us seriously think about who we are and who we should be. Especially, it must be revealed to us that a true teaching and a practical method exist, enabling anyone who sincerely follows it to become a free and independent individual, a real man or woman (without quotation marks).

But first we must realize that we are only slaves to external stimuli, and therefore in prison. If we do not know this, we will not make any effort to escape and become free. When we realize it and desire our freedom, then and only then, will we have the possibility to escape, to free ourselves.

At the conclusion of *Beelzebub's Tales to His Grandson*, Hassein asks Beelzebub, given the unfortunate state of human beings on earth, how they might be helped to perceive reality and to understand who they really are. Beelzebub answers with the hope that if every human being could somehow keep in front of them the inevitability of his/her own death and the death of everyone around him/her, then this might destroy the egoism that is the hallmark of the personality and that prevents realization of the truth.

Sadly, it is only too true that almost all those whom Gurdjieff calls "man" or "woman" (in quotation marks) are unaware that they are in prison, the prison of identification. Consequently, these "men" and "women" do not make effort, and most of them are satisfied with the security of being in prison. Tragically, most do not even know they are imprisoned. If, as Beelzebub suggests, we could continually be cognizant of our mortality, we would then be inspired to work for our freedom.

This introduction to Gurdjieff's teaching might give the impression that the Work is something that can be written about, talked about, and engaged in as an ordinary endeavor. For the most part we do use the techniques suggested in a straightforward manner to approach reality. But a finger pointing at the moon is itself not the moon. What we are after is something quite subtle, and while words can point to it, the words are not it. Whatever we can put words to, is not it. When we speak of knowing who we are, whether we call it Endlessness as Gurdjieff prefers, or by any other word, that is not it, at least not in any way to which words can be put. It can be experienced, as in Thomas Merton's attempted description given in the lesson on meditation. But as Merton says, "As soon as you attempt to make words or thoughts about it you are excluded." [30]

Ultimately, we are confronted with the mystery of being:

> The root of the mystery of being lies at the root of the awareness which perceives the universe. Every human being is human by virtue of that awareness. Every human being is or can be aware that he is aware. When that self-awareness is traced to its inner source, then only can the identity of the individual with the universal be found, then only can the mystery of being be solved.[31]

Appendix 1

Who are you Master Gurdjieff? A speculative enqiry 32

a. What makes a master?

Students of Gurdjieff's teaching have often asked themselves and others: "Who is Gurdjieff?" The very power of his practical teaching and the elegance of the cosmology he proposed have made it seem that Gurdjieff was no ordinary human being. It is not intended here to assert Gurdjieff's status, but rather to suggest possibilities inferred from his own writings and the writings of others in relation to this matter.

Students who knew Gurdjieff personally were overwhelmed by the power radiating from him. One of those students, René Zuber, a French journalist, became a student of Gurdjieff in Paris during World War II. There, under the Nazi occupation, Zuber, along with others, took part in the teaching sessions that Gurdjieff led at his Paris apartment.

On one occasion, Zuber asked the question: "Monsieur, who are you, then? Are you a true master or a false one? I never board a ship without being perfectly sure of the journey and the identity of the captain." [33] Zuber went on to write a book, as did so many of Gurdjieff's students, and he titled his book with that very question: "Who are you Monsieur Gurdjieff?"

In his book, Zuber says that the question burned in him, and he answered it in this way:

> Who could pride himself on ever having met Gurdjieff? A master meets you for the sole purpose of showing you the direction, the way to the inner master which is called conscience. He helps you to discover that you are already its subject, but that you were not aware of it. And then he disappears. He melts into the sky as the mountain does the moment you believe you have set foot on it ...[34]

In *Beelzebub's Tales to His Grandson*, Gurdjieff refers to many masters. The ones with whom we are familiar have been the disseminators of wisdom, and whose teachings have formed the great religions. Krishna, Moses, Gautama, Jesus, and Muhammad are among the well known masters mentioned by Gurdjieff. In describing the taking of birth by such a being, Gurdjieff says:

> Saintly Individuals sometimes actualize within the presence of some terrestrial three-brained being, a "definitized" conception of a sacred Individual in order that

he, having become a terrestrial being with such a presence, may there on the spot "orientate himself" and give to the process of their ordinary being existence ... a corresponding new direction ...[35]

Was Gurdjieff one of these saintly individuals actualized within the presence of an ordinary human being? About Gurdjieff's mastership, the Hindu monk and Indian guru, Sri Madhava Ashish, had this to say:

The Master is one with the spirit. He exemplifies the final attainment. He is what is as yet only a partially realized potential in your own being. You can "recognize" him only to the extent that you can feel the responses in your essence when like answers to like. G. [Gurdjieff]is a Master. [36]

b. Blavatsky and the concept of masters

The concept of the master is an ancient one, but in the context of René Zuber's question, it echoes back to Helena P. Blavatsky, who founded the Theosophical Society in 1875, presumably upon the instructions of her two teachers whom she claimed to have met in Tibet years earlier.

Blavatsky called her two teachers, Morya and Koot Hoomi, "masters." She said that she first met the master Morya in the flesh in London in 1851. She said that Koot Hoomi was a Kashmiri Brahman educated in Europe and that Morya was a Rajput prince, and that they were part of a brotherhood of evolved beings whom she called the masters of wisdom, and who mostly lived in Tibet. Blavatsky also described these masters as imbued with extraordinary powers as the result of their evolutionary development through the experience of a series of lifetimes, and among these powers was the ability to communicate with her psychically at a distance. She herself was known to possess highly developed psychical faculties.

Blavatsky was fluent in several languages and was a prolific writer. [37] Among her accomplishments was the writing of her magnum opus, *The Secret Doctrine*, published in 1888. Blavatsky said that she received help from Morya and Koot Hoomi who, she claimed, had psychically transmitted much of the content to her.

The Secret Doctrine, published in two volumes, purports to be a theoretical description of the universe or macrocosm in volume one, and a theoretical description of the human being, or microcosm, in volume two. In this sense, man, the microcosm, is a reflection of the universe, the macrocosm, constructed under the same great laws of world-creation and world-maintenance, and differing from the macrocosm only relatively, that is, only in terms of scale.

In the two published volumes of *The Secret Doctrine*, written toward the end of the nineteenth century, there are statements indicating that additional portions of the teaching introduced in these volumes would be given out by the masters in the twentieth century. Blavatsky tells us that there are important parts of the teaching not disclosed by her in the first two volumes, especially concerning practical work.

> ... these two volumes should form for the student a fitting prelude for Volumes III and IV. Until the rubbish of the ages is cleared away from the minds of the Theosophists to whom these volumes are dedicated, it is impossible that the more practical teaching contained in the Third Volume should be understood. Consequently, it entirely depends upon the reception with which Volumes I and II will meet at the hands of Theosophists and Mystics, whether these last two volumes will ever be published, though they are *almost* completed. [38]

> In Volume III of this work (the said volume and the IVth being almost ready) a brief history of all the great adepts known to the ancients and the moderns in their chronological order will be given, as also a bird's eye view of the Mysteries, their birth, growth, decay, and final death – in Europe. [39]

> In that volume (III) a brief recapitulation will be made of all the principal adepts known to history. [40]

> In Century the Twentieth some disciple more informed, and far better fitted, may be sent by the Masters of Wisdom to give final and irrefutable proofs that there exists a Science called *Gupta-Vidya* (Esoteric or Secret Science); and that, like the once-mysterious sources of the Nile, the source of all religions and philosophies now known to the world has been for many ages forgotten and lost to men, is at last found. [41]

The elders of the Theosophical Society in the early part of the twentieth century, then under the leadership of Annie Besant, were not unmindful of Blavatsky's prediction about a disciple being sent by the masters of wisdom. Besant spoke incessantly of the imminent coming of the world teacher. Benefiting from the psychic insights of her colleague Charles Leadbeater, they discovered the young Jiddu Krishnamurti, the son of a worker at the Theosophical Society headquarters in India, and saw in him the fulfillment of the prophecy. Subsequent events showed Krishamurti to be a serious teacher.

Some students claim that Krishnamurti's discourses, given largely in the form of dialogues, constitute the practical teaching anticipated in the already issued volumes of *The Secret Doctrine*. Others cannot find in them the "how to" given out in a usable form. Krishnamurti himself seems to have settled the issue, disclaiming any mantle of authority as the predicted disciple in his arguably most important speech "Truth is a Pathless Land," given before thousands of Theosophists in Holland in 1929.

c. Gurdjieff enters the scene

Let us now look at Gurdjieff's position when he appeared in Russia in 1907, coming into the public eye in Moscow in 1912, and consider his actions over the ensuing decades. Let us assume for a moment that Gurdjieff is a master, having taken incarnation in the body of a Greek/Armenian child in accordance with Theosophical theory. This theory holds that a master comes back into incarnation in a new child, rapidly recapitulates the knowledge gained in previous incarnations, and then proceeds to teach anew. If so, then like other masters recounted in *Beelzebub's Tales to His Grandson*, such as Krishna, Moses, Gautama, Jesus, and Muhammad, Gurdjieff had taken incarnation to help guide relatively unconscious humanity in the twentieth century and into the twenty-first.

Gurdjieff, through his Theosophical contacts, was undoubtedly aware of Blavatsky's predictions in *The Secret Doctrine*. P.D. Ouspensky, whom he met in 1913, and who became his most prominent student, was already well known in Russian Theosophical circles. A.R. Orage, the acclaimed British literary editor and eventually Gurdjieff's American representative, was a public speaker for the Theosophical Society in England. Two other students, also Theosophists, Maud Hoffman and Trevor Barker, were heavily involved in the publication of the Mahatma Letters, as we shall see later. We can readily assume from these and other contacts that Gurdjieff knew a great deal about Theosophy and the Theosophical movement. Let us further assume he wanted to give the world indications that he is the teacher predicted in *The Secret Doctrine*, who will bring the practical teaching. How does he do it?

Of course, he actually brought the practical teaching. That was his job. It is why he came back into incarnation. The practical teaching is, according to *The Secret Doctrine*, as much oral as it is written. Gurdjieff gave it out orally and piecemeal to Ouspensky and others in the early Russian groups. Ouspensky recognized this and realized "that a great deal of time must pass before (he) could tell (himself) that (he) could outline the whole system correctly." [42] Eventually, Ouspensky outlined the system and wrote it down as he understood it, however incompletely. This written account, *In Search of the Miraculous* (formerly *Fragments of an Unknown Teaching*) was published only after the deaths of both Ouspensky in 1947 and Gurdjieff in 1949.

By the 1920s, Gurdjieff was certainly aware of Krishnamurti's selection by the Theosophists as the incarnation of the new world teacher. He could hardly stand in opposition to this. It would have appeared unseemly and he would have been accused of being self-serving. What does he do? He begins to write.

d. Writing *Beelzebub's Tales to His Grandson*

Gurdjieff had, by now, after the major auto accident he suffered in 1924, which determined that he would have to close his residential school, dedicated himself to writing. He now writes the intentionally abstruse *Beelzebub's Tales to his Grandson*. This book is, first of all, a practical guide to the Work, giving specific practical exercises for the purpose of working on oneself, along with presenting an elegant cosmology, and hundreds of criticisms of the behavior of human beings from ancient times and into the twentieth century.

But Gurdjieff also wrote into *Beelzebub's Tales to His Grandson* a scenario that would fulfill Blavatsky's prediction. He did this by creating, as a primary character, a great scientist who appears as a Saturnian bird, Gornahoor Harharkh. This bird scientist helped Beelzebub (or Gurdjieff) to construct a telescope on the planet Mars, by which he was able to observe the happenings on earth. In this way he is able to give, in Blavatsky's words, "a bird's eye view [through the telescope] of the Mysteries, their birth, growth, decay, and final death" [43] as Blavatsky predicted. For good measure Gurdjieff recites in his book what Blavatsky termed "a brief history of all the great adepts known to the ancients and the moderns in their chronological order", [44] also as Blavatsky had predicted. Gurdjieff need not have done any of this and could still have given out the practical teachings in *Beelzebub's Tales to His Grandson*. That he chose this scenario in fulfillment of Blavatsky's predictions is highly suggestive of Gurdjieff's intent to fulfill *The Secret Doctrine* prophecy.

e. The Mahatma Letters connection [45]

While the scenario of *Beelzebub's Tales to His Grandson* strongly suggests Gurdjieff's efforts to make it fit in with Blavatsky's predictions, there is additional evidence of Gurdjieff's connection with Blavatsky's teachers, whom she called her "masters." This is the curious affair of letters written by two of the masters and their subsequent publication.

When Blavatsky moved the headquarters of the Theosophical Society from New York City, where she founded it in 1875, to Mumbai (Bombay), in 1879, and then subsequently to Adyar, a suburb of Chennai (Madras), India, her activities came to the attention of the British establishment that then ruled India. Among the more prominent Englishmen who became interested in Blavatsky and her work were Alfred P. Sinnett, editor at the time of *The Pioneer*, then the largest English language newspaper in India, and Allen O. Hume, a career governmental official, Secretary to the British Government of India and founder of the Indian National Congress.

In 1880, having become aware of Blavatsky's reputed psychical powers and hearing of her connection with her two teachers, the masters Morya and Koot Hoomi, the Englishmen wished, especially Sinnett, to be put in contact with these teachers. Blavatsky was doubtful but nevertheless agreed to try, attempting to psychically transmit the content of a letter written by Sinnett to the master, Koot Hoomi. To

Blavatsky's surprise, Sinnett received a written reply from Koot Hoomi. This reply was presumably transmitted by occult means, and from that an ongoing correspondence ensued. The letters themselves are a combination of personal correspondence between the masters, and Sinnett and Hume, as well as documents, in the form of letters, containing substantive occult teachings.

In all, a total of 148 letters were received from these masters between 1880 and 1884 by Sinnett and Hume, after which the correspondence stopped. Shortly thereafter, Sinnett retired and returned from India to England, taking the letters with him. In England, in 1910, he met Maud Hoffman, a Theosophist and American Shakespearean actress, who would become his executrix, upon his death in 1921. Thus, in 1921, Hoffman became the "owner" of the 148 letters written by the masters Morya and Koot Hoomi to Sinnett and Hume, and she decided that they should be made public. She chose another member of the Theosophical Society, Alfred Trevor Barker, to edit the letters for publication. The letters became spoken of and known as "The Mahatma Letters." (In 1939, the actual letters were given by Hoffman to the British Library where they they can now be viewed.)

During that same year, 1921, P.D. Ouspensky arrived in London from Istanbul (Constantinople) and began giving public lectures on Gurdjieff's teaching at the Theosophical Society. Hoffman and Barker attended these lectures and became Ouspensky's students. Shortly thereafter, in early 1922, Gurdjieff arrived in London en route, eventually, to France, where he would settle after the extensive travels that brought him over the Caucasus and out of Russia. Hoffman and Barker met Gurdjieff during his London stay, and transferred from Ouspensky's group to become students of Gurdjieff. In the autumn of 1922, Gurdjieff went on to France, where he leased the Chateau du Prieuré des Basses Loges at Fontainebleau-Avon as the site for his residential school. Hoffman and Barker soon followed from England, along with others who would help Gurdjieff prepare the school to receive students. Barker, while staying at the Prieuré along with Hoffman, was editing the Mahatma Letters in preparation for their publication.

During the following year, 1923, Hoffman wrote an extensive article for the New York Times, detailing the sacred dances and other work in which she participated with Gurdjieff and his other students at the Prieuré. They were sensationalized in the press as the "forest philosophers." (This article appeared in the New York Times on 10 February 1924.) Meanwhile, Barker completed his editing of the Mahatma letters and these were published by the Theosophical Society in December 1923.

It can be seen from this account that there was a much closer relationship between people in the Theosophical movement and people who were students of Gurdjieff than has generally been supposed. In several instances, the same people were members of both movements. It also shows that Gurdjieff was on the scene while the work of editing the Mahatma Letters was going on. It would be naive to think that Gurdjieff knew nothing about the work with the Mahatma Letters in which his students, Hoffman and Barker, were engaged, from February 1922 through September 1923, when the letters were being edited for publication by the Theosophical Society.

This brings us full circle back to Blavatsky who, in a letter to an early member of the Theosophical Society, psychically foreshadowed the coming of Gurdjieff.

f. Blavatsky's prediction: an instructor in dancing

Dr Kenneth Walker, an eminent London physician, surgeon, and professor of medicine, was a student of Gurdjieff's teaching under Ouspensky. He continued to work with and to write about the teaching until his death in 1966, publishing several books. In his book, *A Study of Gurdjieff's Teaching*, Walker tells of Gurdjieff's expertise as a teacher of sacred dance. Through such dances (which have become known as the Gurdjieff Movements) along with special music which he brought with him when he emerged in Russia, Gurdjieff also brought his teaching. Gurdjieff saw this as another method, suited to particular types of people who, through participation in these special dance and exercise techniques, could be helped to attain an experiential state of heightened consciousness. Walker makes the following statement:

> Indeed, in most European circles Gurdjieff was regarded not so much as a philosopher, but as one of the greatest living experts on the sacred dances of the East. What may be of interest to many readers is that in a letter written by Madame Blavatsky to one of the early members of the Theosophical Society, she foretells that the next great teacher of Eastern ideas in Europe will be an instructor in Oriental dancing. [46]

To help draw this connection for the reader who is not yet familiar with *Beelzebub's Tales to His Grandson*, we are reminded by Gurdjieff of a title he attributed to himself at the end of the first chapter of the book. He called himself, "simply, a 'Teacher of Dancing.' " [47]

Appendix 2

Gurdjieff and the study of dreams

a.The importance of accessing the subconscious

Whether the study of dreams is truly a part of Gurdjieff's teaching is controversial. This is because of two talks Gurdjieff gave in 1923 and 1924, in which he mentioned dreams.[48] Confusion about what Gurdjieff meant in these talks have turned many students away from the study of their dreams. This is unfortunate because a close examination of Gurdjieff's teaching reveals the importance he attached to the need to access the subconscious. The most widely used tool for this purpose is the interpretation of symbolism in dreams, and the discerning student will want to avail him or herself of this important tool. The use of this tool is not new, and accounts of dream interpretation go back thousands of years. One need only look at *The Old Testament* to discover their wide use in biblical times.

To understand Gurdjieff's teaching about the importance of accessing the subconscious, we need to understand what he meant by the various terms that he used to describe what is in our ordinary everyday consciousness and what has been suppressed into the subconscious.

Gurdjieff defines a human being as being divided into two primary components: personality and essence.

He speaks of three lower centers: the moving-instinctive, the emotional, and the intellectual centers as constituting the personality. Sometimes he spoke of the moving-instinctive center as itself being composed of three centers: the moving, the instinctive, and the sex centers. These three (or five) lower centers represent the growth, education, and experience of this lifetime.

The two higher centers of which Gurdjieff speaks, the higher emotional center and the higher intellectual center, form our essence, our essential and higher nature. These higher centers are synonymous with two other interchangeable Gurdjieffian terms, objective consciousness and objective conscience. Gurdjieff tells us that the higher centers are always transmitting wisdom to us, only we cannot hear them because, as he explains in *Beelzebub's Tales to His Grandson*, objective conscience has been suppressed into the subconscious.

It is important to understand that essence is who we really are and is eternal, whereas personality is time-bound, arising at birth and ending at death or shortly thereafter. In describing who we really are, Gurdjieff has used interchangeably a variety of terms: Endlessness, essence, higher centers, objective conscience, and objective consciousness among others. The coating of the spiritual body, which Gurdjieff tells us is necessary, refers to our ability to stand in essence rather than in personality.

In a talk given at the Prieuré in January, 1923, Gurdjieff said that a person's centers never sleep, and that what we regard as memory, attention, and observation is simply the observation of one of the centers by another.[49]

The observation of one center by another is accomplished by connections between the lower centers. When the connections are broken, sleep ensues, and the more connections that are broken, the deeper is the sleep. Gurdjieff spoke of several degrees of sleep, from the lightest to the deepest depending upon how many connections are broken. When we sleep and dream, at least one of the connections between centers is not broken. When the unbroken connections are between only the lower centers, these result in unnecessary half-dream and mundane dream states. But if the unbroken connection(s) are between the higher centers and the lower centers, we can then receive wisdom from the higher centers. Therefore, while it is important that the connections between the lower centers are broken so that we can sleep briefly but relatively deeply, we shall want the connections between the higher and lower centers to remain unbroken during our night sleep.

The importance of receiving wisdom from the higher centers is recognized in the writings of two of Gurdjieff's most prominent students, Maurice Nicoll and Margaret Anderson, [50] and most importantly, in Gurdjieff's own writing.

Dr Maurice Nicoll was a prominent British psychiatrist and protégé of C.G. Jung, who went to study under Gurdjieff at the Prieuré in 1922. Nicoll is best known for the talks on the Gurdjieff teaching that he gave to groups of students over a 12-year period from 1941 to 1953. These are published in the five-volume set: *Psychological Commentaries on the Teaching of G.I. Gurdjieff and P.D. Ouspensky.*

As a psychiatrist, Nicoll was familiar with the use of dreams for accessing the subconscious and particularly with Jung's work on dream symbolism. [51] Nicoll mentions dreams in five of his commentaries, and he tries to make clear the distinction between mundane dreams and significant dream messages coming from higher centers. Mundane dreams with no particular significance are, as Gurdjieff says, nothing more than one center observing another. These are the lower centers observing one another with at least one of the connections between these centers remaining unbroken during night sleep.

But Nicoll pointed out that there are significant dreams and that these significant dreams come from the higher emotional and higher intellectual centers. In this sense, the higher in us imparts wisdom to our ordinary waking consciousness.

> There are intellectual dreams, emotional dreams, sexual dreams, moving and instinctive dreams, and there are also dreams that come from the centers we do not use – i.e. higher emotional and higher intellectual centres ... Do you remember what the Work teaches about higher centres? It teaches that higher centres are fully developed in us and are always transmitting meaning to us only we cannot hear them ... Very often G. used to say that we must listen to ourselves ... [but] we listen to the crudest 'I's ...yet all the time there are influences, so clearly expressed in the diagram of the Ray of Creation, that are trying to touch us, and make us understand better, and cure us of our life-maladies and so lead us to our own inner development. Sometimes these influences reach us in the form of dreams.[52]

In listing the highlights of Gurdjieff's teaching, Margaret Anderson in *The Unknowable Gurdjieff*, includes the study of dreams about which she writes, "Study your dreams. There is a self-contained energy left over in one of the centers." [53]

Gurdjieff places vast importance on our need to access the subconscious so that we can receive the wisdom of the higher centers. He explains the importance of accessing the subconscious in chapters 25–28 of *Beelzebub's Tales to His Grandson*, through the saga of Ashiata Shiemash.

Unlike other widely known teachers around whom traditional religions have formed, Ashiata Shiemash is unknown to us. According to Gurdjieff, he took incarnation in a Sumerian boy born in Pispascana, near to Babylon, some seven centuries before the height of the Babylonian civilization. This would be about 2400 B.C. There is no historical evidence for the existence of such a being, so we may assume that Ashiata Shiemash is an allegorical figure created by Gurdjieff to propound a particular aspect of his teaching.

Although Ashiata Shiemash's teaching was extant for only a few generations and was eventually lost to humanity, he was, according to Gurdjieff, the only "messenger from above" who succeeded in creating conditions through which human beings on earth could live normal lives.

Central to the teaching in the Ashiata Shiemash allegory is the idea that objective conscience has been suppressed into the subconscious. In the Ashiata Shiemash chapters Gurdjieff uses the term objective-conscience as equivalent to objective consciousness, the fourth state of human consciousness, or enlightenment. But, as

Gurdjieff tells us through the words of Ashiata Shiemash, objective conscience has been suppressed into the subconscious.

> The factor which ought to engender that being-impulse on which the whole psyche of beings of a three-brained system is in general based, and which impulse exists under the name of Objective-Conscience, is not yet atrophied in them, but remains in their presences almost in its primordial state.

> Thanks to the abnormally established conditions of external ordinary being-existence existing here, this factor has gradually penetrated and become embedded in that consciousness which is here called "subconsciousness," in consequence of which it takes no part whatever in the functioning of their ordinary consciousness ...

> I ... understood ... that if the functioning of that being-factor still surviving in their common-presences were to participate in the general functioning of that consciousness of theirs in which they pass their daily, as they say here, "waking-existence," only then would it still be possible to save the contemporary three-brained beings here ...

> I decided to consecrate the whole of myself from that time on to the creation here of such conditions that the functioning of the "sacred-conscience," still surviving in their subconsciousness, might gradually pass into the functioning of their ordinary consciousness.[54]

The good news is that because of its suppression into the subconscious, objective conscience is not yet atrophied in us. But because objective conscience, the higher centers in us, has been suppressed into the subconscious, it takes no part whatever in the functioning of our ordinary consciousness. Our work, therefore, is to access the subconscious so that objective conscience or the higher centers can impart its wisdom to us.

Gurdjieff said that his teaching differs from many others in that it affirms that the higher centers exist in man and are fully developed.[55] Because the higher centers are objective and not identified with the personality, they can objectively show us the identifications with personality characteristics, which we need to observe in ourself and from which we need to free ourself.

It is identification that blocks us from objectivity, from objective consciousness. Gurdjieff warns us specifically of the tyranny of identification and calls it one of our most terrible foes. He says that it is necessary to see and to study identification to its very roots in oneself.[56]

Identification, from which we must free ourselves, is the flow of our attention into "desire" and into its counterpart, "fear," in all their myriad forms. He tells us that we must consciously assist non-desires to predominate over desires.[57]

Gurdjieff also tells us that freeing ourselves from identification with desires and fears requires cleaning our psyche of those identifications, but in order to undertake this cleaning in a rational way, we need to see what needs to be cleaned and where and how to do it.[58]

Studying identifying to its very roots in oneself and cleaning our machine of the dirt that has clogged it in the course of our lives is work of a psychological nature. For this reason, it is necessary to use psychological tools, and in particular, psychological tools to access the subconscious so that we can bring the wisdom of objective conscience into our ordinary consciousness.

Psychology has developed a variety of tools to access the subconscious. These include, for example, hypnotism of which Gurdjieff had been a practitioner, psychological probing, and the analysis of dreams.

The analysis of our dreams is especially useful because it is something in which we can each engage without reliance upon an outside analyst or hypnotist. Because objective conscience is suppressed into the subconscious, it speaks to us through dream in symbolic form to avoid censorship by the personality, as is well known in modern psychology. With some textual guidance, based on the principles of modern psychology, and our own good common sense, we can learn to interpret these symbols. When we learn to interpret our dream symbols, we are able to receive objective teaching coming from our higher centers, from objective conscience.

b. The development of a dream theory[59]

It is known that Gurdjieff talked privately with some pupils, such as Margaret Anderson, about the use of dream symbols to access the subconscious. Other pupils like Maurice Nicoll have come forward to affirm their importance. But we have no published accounts of specific instruction that Gurdjieff gave to particular students about how to go about the study of dreams.

We turn, therefore, to a follower and exponent of Gurdjieff's teaching, Sri Madhava Ashish (1920–1997) who, together with his mentor, Sri Krishna Prem (1897–1965), developed esoteric dream analysis theory, based on Gurdjieffian teaching and Jungian psychological principles.

Neither Ashish nor Prem are names well known to most western students of Gurdjieff's teaching, although they are well known to Indian admirers as having been exponents of Gurdjieff's teaching. Over the years a surprising number of Western students of the Gurdjieff teaching had made their way up to the Mirtola ashram in the Indian Himalayas to visit these two men, Englishmen who had become Indian Hindu monks. Visitng luminaries have included Olga de Hartmann, Philip Lavastine, Bernard Courtenay Mayor, Ethel Merston, Lizelle Reymond, and Laurence Rosenthal. Jeanne de Salzmann met Madhava Ashish in Delhi and P.L. Travers was a regular correspondent.

We all, Madhava Ashish once said, "drink from the same cup of truth." He and Krishna Prem always referred to Gurdjieff with great reverence, calling him "the great Russian Boddhisattva" after the country in which he first appeared publicly. Madhava Ashish seemed to know Gurdjieff intimately as did Krishna Prem, although neither had ever met Gurdjieff in the flesh.

Many other lesser known students of Gurdjieff's teaching including this writer have visited Mirtola or otherwise corresponded. On one occasion, in speaking of dreams, Ashish said:

> Your dreams are important. Begin to pay attention to them. Your dreams will tell you things about yourself that you have buried too deeply to uncover directly. It's another way to "know thyself," that famous injunction of the Delphic oracle about which Gurdjieff speaks.[60]

While we may, at the outset, perceive a dream message as coming from someone external to ourselves, whether it appears to be Gurdjieff or Jesus, or we call it the higher centers, eventually we come to understand that the higher centers are us. They are not the collection of tissues and memories that we call "me," but rather our essential being which Gurdjieff also calls the spiritual body.

Gurdjieff tells us that it is necessary to crystallize or coat the spiritual body. This does not mean that we do not have a spiritual body. It is more accurate to say that we do not stand in the spiritual body or essence, because we do not know who we are.

Coating the spiritual body is the work of changing our viewpoint so that we stand in essence rather than in personality. Gurdjieff refers to this as entering the Holy Planet Purgatory, and of it he says, "only he may enter here who puts himself in the position of the other results of my labors." [61] Coating of the spiritual body is only possible when we stand in essence rather than in personality, and it is connected with two additional requirements for coating the spiritual body. Gurdjieff enumerates these as engaging in "conscious labor" and "intentional suffering." [62] All these requirements necessitate intentional effort.

Through this intentional effort, we eventually come to see that in essence there is no separation between any of us. We are ourselves and at the same time we are all each other. In speaking of beings who have already realized this, Madhava Ashish said:

> Any one of those beings (if it has any meaning to speak of these being more than one essential being) can look out through the eyes of any existing form that has eyes. There is a series of masks, shaped in the familiar forms of Gurdjieff, Jesus, the Buddha, Maurya, etc., so that idiots like us can recognize them, through which the one power can communicate with us.[63]

Of our role in all this, he went on to say:

> To understand G and his brethren one has to become one of them. How can I understand someone who literally has a dimension to his being that I either lack or have only in an undeveloped form? That won't stop me from trying to understand, but I should know that the most important part of my effort to understand must lie in the effort to understand myself and to find the "higher Self" in myself. [64]

It is because of this that the study of our dreams is so important. The higher centers are always transmitting wisdom to us, only we usually cannot hear it. Through the interpretation of our dream symbols, we allow the wisdom of the higher centers to pass into the functioning of our ordinary consciousness.

c. Psychology and the use of dream symbolism

There is a distinction between the use by psychologists of the analytical tools of dream symbolism analysis for helping people to deal with their mundane lives, and the use of the same tools to recognize teachings from our higher centers. Madhava Ashish explained the importance of the esoteric use of modern psychology as follows:

> The psychological theory of dreaming has, of course, been popular since Freud. This still holds good. What is lacking in most current dream theory, as it is lacking in the current world view, is the presence of a spiritual centre and a universal view to which the personal psychic patterns can be related, and which gives significance to the person and his struggles with his nature.[65]

> Modern psychology (the work of Freud, Jung & company) in general adopts the materialistic standpoint, especially in its psychiatric form, and so denies the real existence of all that is represented by the word soul. Ancient psychology is the science of the soul. In this sense, Buddhism is known as the first psychological religion, because Buddha taught the causes of sorrow and their removal in terms of states of mind and feeling. Thus, every teacher of the inner work has been a psychologist. Our difficulty lies in the fact that modern psychology has achieved

remarkable insights into the working of the subconscious mind-feeling complex and the effects it has on the feelings and thoughts we are conscious of. All this is of immense usefulness to anyone struggling to control his mind, to deal with negative emotions, to distinguish between his essential awareness and the sort of awareness that is present in what G calls "sleep." But we cannot afford to use this knowledge without distinguishing it from the uses to which modern psychology puts it …

In our field we can treat as fact Freud's dictum that dreams are the royal road into the unconscious, but we do not therefore have to accept Freud's theories about ego and id, etc., or to accept the academic flavor that dulls so much of his work. Freud did not discover dreams; he gave some structure to the area of (un)consciousness from which dreams (and much of our compulsive behavior) take their rise. Dreams and visions have provided seekers with data for their search since the beginning of time.

Our work is so difficult that we need every bit of help we can get. It really does not matter where or from whom we take help, provided that we have enough intelligence and a clear enough view of our goal to be able to take help that is consonant with our aim and to reject those components that are contrary to it.

It is obvious that danger lies in any inability to distinguish between the consonant and the contrary. The prestige of the modern psychologists is such that they are thought so profoundly wise that we must either believe them totally or not at all. On the other hand, we ourselves want to use their perceptions but to reject their conclusions …

In respect of modern psychology there are at least three classes of people we are concerned with:

Firstly, there are the pathological cases, people who are so disturbed that they are out of touch with reality and, at most, can be helped to lead "normal" lives. Such people often feel attracted to the inner path, but it is dangerous to have anything to do with them. They should be advised to seek medical/psychological help.

Secondly, there are the people who may have considerable potential for the Work, but who are so tangled up with traumas, compulsions or emotional blocks of one sort or another that they cannot work with any sense of real purpose and joy. If we ourselves cannot provide the insights to help them, they may benefit from psychoanalysis, psychotherapy, etc. In this case we try to recommend a practitioner who is personally sympathetic to the Work. He will not aim to turn a confused patient into a well adapted moron.

Thirdly, we have the reasonably well-adapted people who appear to be fit for the Work, but whom anyone can see to be tied up in the usual knots of parental "fixations," inhibited emotions, insecurities and all the rest of the desires and fears which make control of the mind so difficult a task that many of them despair. These are the ones who can benefit from psychological insight, but who should not be sent to professional practitioners. In order to qualify for practice, professionals have had to subscribe to the non-spiritual ethic of their particular schools, and this rubs off on their patients.

We also have to guard against the mistaken assumption that psychoanalysis can be equated with the Work. We want the analytical tools to help us in our work – specifically to help free us from the compulsions which, unless seen and dealt with, control our minds. But the Work itself is something quite different. Similarly, analysis helps us to still the mind, but a still mind is only a step towards transcending the mind. I must also add that there is no reason to suppose that psychological qualifications would be useful to a group leader. Just as wide reading of mysticism, mythology, religion, and other subjects is of value to anyone in this Work, so is a familiarity with modern psychology. But one no more needs academic qualification in modern psychology to help people with their psychological problems vis-à-vis the inner Work, than one needs to be a priest or a professor to be inspired by mysticism and myth.

It also seems to be a fact that modern psychology suits the psyche of modern man; and this is partly because it breaks through the old conventions in much the same way that modern life has broken from the old conventions. However, it is also plain that men have followed this path throughout the ages without the help of this particular set of insights we call modern psychology. Our point, therefore, is not that psychology is a sine qua non, but that it should not be rejected out of hand or its usefulness denied to people who could benefit from it …

While it is very obvious to anyone who has open eyes that the whole of G's self-remembering, dealing with negative emotions and many other points are strictly psychological in the true sense, there are none so blind as those who refuse to see …

It has to be emphasized that we need the tools, but not the men who fashioned these tools; they use them to help people who are so screwed up that they cannot even manage their daily lives; we intend to use them for liberating our minds from the compulsive forces which act on them.[66]

d. Seven principles of dream analysis

Madhava Ashish had developed a list that he called the seven principles of dream analysis, which he distributed privately to students. These principles emphasize the importance of accessing the subconscious through dream analysis, so that instruction from objective consciousness can pass into the functioning of our ordinary consciousness. Gurdjieff stresses the importance of this in the allegorical teaching of Ashiata Shiemash.

We can all follow these principles of dream analysis. They are tools made up of good common sense, as are the common sense techniques for remembering and recalling dreams. By engaging ourselves in this way, we are following Gurdjieff's instructions, as he put them into the mouth of Ashiata Shiemash, to access the subconscious so that what is suppressed in our subconscious is brought into our ordinary consciousness.

Abbreviating and reformulating these principles for the Western student, they can be stated as follows: [67]

1. Although on occasion dreams can tell us about others, we need to look at them as if they apply only to us. In fact, almost all our dreams do apply only to us. Even if a dream appears to involve another person, we should mainly take the dream as showing us something about ourselves. The other person in the dream is usually a symbol for a characteristic that we need to see in ourselves.

2. The Self (which we are but don't know it) is giving us direction through our dreams and is urging us to growth, maturity, and wholeness.

3. We should take dreams as giving us useful criticism about ourselves, about things in us that need looking at and changing. Dreams often use criticism in a creative way. They reveal truths, hidden factors that have been inhibiting the fullness of life, but in a way that encourages and affirms, frequently providing help towards the resolution of whatever difficulties they reveal, often in witty and unexpected ways. Dreams can also appear to be complimentary, but when they are, they are not necessarily of therapeutic value. The good stuff takes care of itself, so we need not bother congratulating ourselves when our dreams seem to compliment us. We need to see the negative qualities in us that our dreams are trying to show us.

4. We need to be ready to look at the lowest and most disgusting parts of ourselves as shown to us by our dreams. Since the Self (the unchanging real), with which we seek unification, includes everything in the universe and beyond, nothing can be excluded from it. We must look at everything with which we as personalities (our lesser self) identify, for example, all manner of anger, rage, sexual problems, fear, greed, and the whole long list of other personality identifications. We can take as a guide to these identifications whatever features there are in us that capture our attention. We need to let go of all these features of our personality.

5. The purpose of releasing repressed material in us through dream interpretation is not just to help make our lives better here, although it is certainly valuable for that.

These things are blocks to our entering into higher states of consciousness that are the characteristic of unification with the Self.

6. If we take as a hypothesis that our dreams are guided by an intelligence greater and wiser than our ordinary waking state, the intelligence of the Self, we need to honor that intelligence by acting on its guidance. We should not take dreams as ordering us to do something, but if advice is given us through our interpretations, we need to see what the advice is and then act on that advice in an intelligent manner.

7. Everyone dreams. If we claim that we do not dream, it is a question of not making sufficient efforts to remember and record our dreams.

e. Techiques for remembering dreams

Many people complain about this last principle, insisting that they do not dream. Clinical studies have shown this to be false and that everyone does dream. The rapid eye movement (REM) state that we all experience periodically during sleep has been identified as the time of dream activity. What we need are tools to help us to remember our dreams. These are, for the most part, common sense tools like these:

1. Affirm your intention to remember and record dreams before retiring. This mindset causes the mind to more easily remember a dream just as the mindset of determining to awaken at a particular hour usually enables one to do so.

2. Keep paper and pencil or a tape recorder at bedside, and arrange whatever other conditions will facilitate the recording of a dream, a bedside light, for example.

3. Provide sleeping conditions that are not unduly comfortable. Sleeping on a hard mattress and pillow, for example, seems to enhance dream recall.

4. If you read before bedtime, read something spiritual, something connected to the inner work. This turns the mind in the appropriate direction for dream recall.

5. Make the effort to record the dream as soon as you awaken, whether in the middle of the night or in daylight. You can attempt interpretation later. If the dream is not recorded immediately upon awakening, even what appears to be the clearest of dreams will frequently just disappear.

6. Maintain a journal of dreams in order to note recurring themes. The message being sent to us from higher centers to observe a particular personality identification will often repeat in a different dream story if it is not noted and acted upon when first received.

7. Every student of dreams goes through "dry" periods. These are periods when dreams do not seem to come. We already know that we all dream all the time, so

we cannot fall back into the complaint that we are not dreaming. The problem is mainly that our so-called "will" is insufficient. We have become lazy. One of the recommended techniques to help restore our attention to and cognizance of the dreams going on in us is to establish an independent and artificial external "will" that makes a demand upon us to remember our dreams. This external will can be provided by consulting with a trusted advisor who then expects us to report our dreams, or it can be provided by participation in a dream-study group. This is a group of people all working together in trust and confidence who meet periodically and who each present their dreams for the group's help in analyzing them. The periodic meeting makes the demand on us to remember and record dreams so that we have material to bring to the group meeting.

f. Purificatory dreams and noumenal dreams

Not every dream brings a message from higher centers. Many dreams are mundane, generated, for instance, by the spicy pizza eaten before going to bed. Discounting mundane dreams resulting from unbroken connections between the lower centers, significant advisory dreams offering wisdom from the higher centers can be divided into two broad classes: purificatory dreams and noumenal [68] dreams. The distinction between these two classes can be likened to the differences between the cleaning of a window and looking through it.

Understanding and working with the messages contained in purificatory dreams is the cleaning of the window. These dreams show us our identifications, identifications that we may not have noticed. Observing these identifications, usually identifications with negative emotions, begins the process of freeing ourselves from these identifications. As we free ourselves, our window of vision becomes cleaner and clearer.

Noumenal dreams allow us to see through the window of vision when it has been sufficiently cleaned.

The seven principles of dream interpretation enumerated above are directed primarily at the first class of dreams, purificatory dreams. These dreams are seen as teaching coming from the higher centers, objective consciousness, showing us personality identifications that need to be observed and detached from. This is the work of cleaning the window of vision. The second class of dreams are noumenal in the sense that through them we see and experience what Gurdjieff calls the real world.

In the first class of dreams, we see our own reflection, the reflection of our personality and its identification with all its fears and desires. In the second class of dreams, once the window has been cleaned, the mind is quieted and we are aware that we stand in objective consciousness. This is why Gurdjieff said that a man can develop his hidden capacities and powers only by cleaning his machine of the dirt that has clogged it in the course of his life.

g. Noumenal dreams and lucid dreaming

When the window of vision has been sufficiently cleaned through work on oneself, *metanoia* takes place. This is the changing of viewpoint so that we begin to see ourselves not as the personality that has been given one physical body and usually one name. We begin to see ourselves as essence.

In the truly noumenal dream, the dreamer experiences his or her identity with the universal, with Endlessness. In such a dream the dreamer is aware of the dream and is aware of being aware of him or herself in the dream. There is the experience of quiet witnessing by the quieted mind. *Metanoia* will have taken place and changed the viewpoint of the dreamer.

The object of true meditation in which the ordinary mind is completely quieted is the same as is the experience of the noumenal dream. Just as it is possible to experience what Gurdjieff has called objective consciousness in the meditative state, with our mind sufficiently quieted we can enter into objective consciousness through the noumenal dream. Whether in meditation or in the noumenal dream, the meditator/dreamer's viewpoint will have changed. One is no longer dedicated to the inner path only some of the time and following the personality's own selfish interests at other times. The totality of one's nature is brought into harmony with one's perceptions of the nature of the source of being.

One method for entering into the state of the noumenal dream provided, as always, that the window of vision has been sufficiently cleaned, is as follows:

> Attempt to carry waking consciousness into the sleep state. There are various ways and the first is to hold the intention throughout the day and while falling asleep.
>
> Do a lot of physical work during the course of a day. Then being exhausted, instead of lying down to go to sleep, quietly remain sitting up. This may allow the body to actually go to sleep while you are in the sitting position, whereas the conscious mind, functioning through the brain, remains awake. These hypnagogic (between waking and deep sleep) and hypnopompic (between deep sleep and wakening) states, ... are states in which it is especially possible to experience what G calls "the real world" the objectively conscious state. In moments of pre-awakening, one cannot stop the physical body from awakening, but one can maintain the state of self-awareness so that one is free from identification, and then go further.
>
> It may take many weeks or months of effort..

G's relaxation exercises can lead to the same state – body asleep, mind awake. Any real meditation has the same result. Few people recognize this fact, because sleep is a dirty word for meditators.

Don Juan [the teacher of Carlos Castaneda in his books on sorcery] works the other way around, not by carrying waking consciousness through the barrier, but by planning to wake up and stay awake in the dream state – effectively the state of astral projection.[69]

Modern dream researchers have called the awakening to the realization that "this is a dream" by the term "lucid dreaming." But the lucid dreamer (and some people seem to have this natural ability), who has not otherwise cleaned the machine of the dirt that has clogged it all its life, will not recognize the free state of the noumenal dream because the mind is not sufficiently quieted. The dream then becomes purificatory because of the identifications that continue to beset the dreamer.

A common failing of naturally lucid dreamers is the tendency to manipulate the dream because of their personality identifications. Dreams are manipulated to produce a story that is satisfactory to the personality of the dreamer.

We must not manipulate the lucid dream to our liking. Such manipulation distorts the state of content-less witnessing awareness and deprives us of the wisdom and insight that is our true nature.

h. How much sleep do we need?
Students frequently ask the question, "How much sleep to I need?" About this, Gurdjieff said that if our organism is in good order, it needs very little time to manufacture the amount of energy for which sleep is intended. He went on to say that if we could fall asleep at once and awaken from night sleep promptly, we would spend just a third to a quarter of the time that we now spend on these transitional states.[70]

For a person on the path of inner inquiry, four or five hours of sleep is sufficient, with an occasional 10-minute rest once or twice a day. This is in addition to daily periods of meditation, which are as restful as or more restful than ordinary sleep.

Recent medical studies argue that most of us do not get enough sleep. It is clearly different for people in the Work. We can intentionally sleep deeply and briefly and manufacture the needed energy for which sleep is intended. At the same time we can also, with intention, access our dreams and receive wisdom from the higher centers, from objective consciousness, as we learn to interpret our dream symbols following the principles of dream analysis given here.

i. Forming a dream study group

Students who wish to avail themselves of teachings received through the study of their dreams may want to form a dream study group. Such a group meets separately from the typical weekly Gurdjieff study group, because extra time is required to present and discuss dreams. The primary purpose of the group is to provide the external will to actually remember and record dreams. Again, it is a matter of providing an artificial 'will' in substitution for our own lack of real will. Another important purpose is to give the dreamer further insight into the meaning of his or her dreams. Participation with others in a dream study group helps us receive insights. These are not just the dreamer's own insights, but also the insights of the other participants. These insights often show the dreamer his or her continuing identification with so-called negative emotions that the dreamer may have mistakenly assumed to have been gotten rid of through the Work.

Typically, a dream study group will meet weekly, and as few as two or three participants can constitute such a group. If there are more than 10, the group may become unwieldy. Depending upon the number of participants, dream study groups usually meet for between 1 and 2 hours. The following parameters have proved useful for dream study groups organized according to the principles suggested here.

1. Each dreamer brings a recent dream (dreamt within the previous week) to each group session. But it is not necessary that every dreamer's dream be presented at each session.

2. Each dreamer in turn presents his/her dream giving the facts of the dream, the life-event background that may have stimulated the dream story, the emotions felt both within the dream and upon awakening, and the dreamer's opinion of what the dream means.

3. Members of the group may ask questions to clarify the dream in order to understand the content.

4. Discussion of the dream is then opened up to the other participants who respond: "If this were my dream, … " and then give a view of what the dream means. It thus becomes clear to the members of the group that such a response is based upon the projections of the member who is speaking and not necessarily those of the dreamer. Often, but not always, the dreamer has an "ah, ha," a realization that "yes, that really is what the dream means." In theory, this is possible because at the deepest levels of the psyche we are all one. We are all Endlessness.

5. Dreams often reveal sensitive personal information. Therefore, the dreamer as well as the facilitator(s) of the group is entitled to cut off discussion of a dream at any time.

6.   Many dreams open to sexual keys. Participants in a dream study group should be prepared to give sexual interpretations of their dreams and should realize that others commenting upon the dream may give sexual interpretations.

7.   Participants in a dream study group must be prepared to respect each other's privacy. There is tacit agreement that the dreams of participants will not be discussed with others outside the group.

8.   Participants may want to have access to one or more dream-symbol dictionaries. Any dream-symbol dictionary can give the dreamer ideas for the meaning of symbols. But it should be noted that all dream dictionaries with ready-made rule-of-thumb interpretations of the symbols in dreams are not worth very much in themselves. Dreams are symbolic and their symbolism cannot be pigeonholed. Symbols are highly personal, although some archetypal symbols often, but not always, apply to larger groups of humanity, i.e. ethnic, racial, cultural, geographic groups. Nevertheless, any such dictionary will give the dreamer some idea of how someone else has interpreted a dream symbol, usually the dictionary writer's interpretation of his or her own symbol.

9.   The book that many students of dream symbolism have found useful is *Man and his Symbols* by C.G. Jung. This is not a dream dictionary. It is more an explanation of how the psyche of human beings has used symbols in dreams, often the same symbols within groups of humanity, to represent an idea. There are many illustrations of symbols, and many are historic symbols. The principal value lies in an examination of these symbols to understand how they are used by the Self, the higher centers, suppressed into the subconscious, to communicate with the personality.

Appendix 3

Exercises

a. A typical weekly exercise

Typically, at the end of the weekly group meeting, the members will agree upon an exercise that they will undertake to engage in during the forthcoming week. These exercises are designed to help us be self-conscious and to observe the impediments to self-consciousness.

Since this is the Fourth Way, a way in life, the members engage in the exercise while they go about their day-to-day activities, whether in school, in business or profession, at home, or wherever they may be. Because these are inner exercises, no one else need know that the member is engaging in such an exercise. It is better that other people do not know, since it may discomfit them.

By way of example, an exercise may be stated as follows: For this week the exercise is the self-observation of "wiseacring." This term appears numerous times throughout *Beelzebub's Tales to His Grandson*. It is a form of lying in which we pretend to know more than we actually know. The dictionary calls a "wiseacre," one who represents himself or herself to be well-informed or clever, a know-it-all or smart aleck.

This exercise has two parts:

1. Self-observe when we wiseacre to another person. Observe this form of lying in ourselves.

2. Self-observe our emotions when someone else wiseacres to us.

As always, in the moment of self-observation, use the tool of "attention" to divide the attention so as to include the sensation/experience of self in the moment. Use attention to sensation of part or all of the body as the primary tool for this purpose.

The method of self-observation and resulting self-consciousness may be expressed as follows:

> Observe an object. The object can be an external object like a candle or it can be an internal object like an emotional state: i.e. anxiety, fear, internal considering, desire, pride, vanity, etc. See the object. See what is seeing the object. Drop away the object. What is left is that you are seeing or observing what is seeing the object.

In other words, you are aware of being aware. This is true self-remembering or self-awareness, avoiding the trap of illusory self-remembering.[71]

There is a subtle distinction between true self-remembering and illusory self-remembering. True self-remembering requires not only being aware of ourselves in our attention and at the same time including the internal or external object. It also means that we must be aware of being aware of ourselves in the moment. This requires a kind of "backing out" as described in the chapter on meditation. To re-quote Thomas Merton's attempt at description: "A door opens in the center of our being and we seem to fall through it into immense depths." [72] This is rather like an infinite regression within as we "back" further out, ever more detached from the personality. The theory behind the benefit of a group undertaking such an exercise is that the group supplies a kind of "will" that as individuals we assume that we have, but in actuality we do not have.

b. Three categories of exercises

Exercises (or tasks as they are sometimes called) can be divided into three categories.

First there are what are called here, the principal exercises. These are exercises so fundamental to the Work that they must be undertaken always and everywhere. However, in attempting them, we discover that we cannot engage in them always and everywhere. All the time, we forget and this helps us to verify the level of our being. So, it becomes an ideal for us to engage in these exercises. It is these, toward which we strive, and we may call them strivings.

Second, there are the so-called "stop" exercises. These are exercises that remind us in the moment to "stop" and come back to the awareness of ourselves in our attention. These exercises help us to enter self-consciousness, the third state of human consciousness in the Gurdjieff teaching.

Third, there are the many psychological exercises or tasks in which we engage to observe the psychological identifications that keep us from being in the third state of consciousness.

Through self-observation, we are able to verify that we cannot continue any of these three categories of exercises for very long without them becoming mechanical in the sense that we forget to engage in them. It is a demonstration of our inadequate will and the weakness of our attention. Therefore, it is customary in group work to change both the second and third categories of exercises from week to week. The principal exercises, however inadequately we attempt them, must stay with us at least as an ideal, always and everywhere.

The lists that follow in this appendix present keywords suggesting the construction of Fourth Way exercises. Most are taken from suggestions in Gurdjieff's own writings, mainly from *Beelzebub's Tales to His Grandson*. Some page references are given where the particular keyword is used in text, but several of these keywords appear in many places throughout Gurdjieff's writings. Any of these keywords can be used to construct an exercise for self-observation similar to the exercise of the self-observation of wiseacring in the foregoing example of a typical weekly exercise. These lists are not meant to be inclusive but rather to demonstrate the variety of features that can be the subject of a group exercise.

While these exercises are designed as group exercises, we can also engage in them alone. The principal difficulty in attempting them alone is our inability to remember to engage in them without the support and the will that are supplied by the group.

Remember that a group can be as few as two people, and working with others as part of a group, however small, is important. So try to find another person or two or three to work with if you are not part of a larger group.

c. The principal exercises or strivings

Fourth Way exercises have to be varied periodically, often weekly. This is so that they do not become mechanical, thus losing their ability to engender self-consciousness. There are, however, certain principal exercises or strivings to which Gurdjieff gives special emphasis and which, therefore, should be practiced always and everywhere. These include the five enumerated being-obligolnian strivings (page 386 of *Beelzebub's Tales to His Grandson*) plus at least an additional seven exercises or strivings, as shown below. Any additional strivings or exercises that the student feels should be practiced always and everywhere may be added to this list. All pages refer to *Beelzebub's Tales to His Grandson*, except the last entry.

Keywords	Page
Striving to provide only what is necessary for the planetary body	386
Striving for self-perfection in the sense of being	386
Striving to understand the laws of world-creation and world-maintenance	386
Striving to pay for our arising and individuality as quickly as possible	386
Striving to assist the most rapid perfecting of other beings	385
Striving to watch the reflection of the splendor of the sunrise every day	78
Striving to meditate every day	355
Striving to consciously labor	792
Striving to intentionally suffer	792
Striving to put ourselves in the position of others	1164

Keywords	Page
Striving to be cognizant of the inevitability of ours and others' deaths (Gurdjieff, *Beelzebub's Tales to His Grandson*)	1183
Striving to manifest "as if" we already stand in objective consciousness (Gurdjieff, *Life is real only then, when "I am"*)	132–136

d. Examples of the reminding and "stop" exercises

Certain Fourth Way exercises are simply reminders to help us to be conscious of being conscious of ourselves in the moment. Some of these remind us so suddenly that we can call them "stop" exercises. The following examples are illustrative (with references, where available, to books by Gurdjieff or Ouspensky), but do not constitute a comprehensive list of reminding and "stop" exercises, and students are encouraged to experiment with the wide range of possible variations.

Keywords	Page
Acting: being a conscious actor (Gurdjieff, *Views from the Real World*)	176–178
Animal noise (i.e. barking, chirping, crowing, mewing) (Gurdjieff, *Beelzebub's Tales to His Grandson*)	223
Appointment at a specific time	
Bedside	
Brushing teeth	
Constructive imagination for example, imagining a vibration when I say, "I am, I can, I wish" (Gurdjieff, *Life is real only then, when "I am"*)	132–136
Death, the cognizance of its inevitability, i.e. use someone's death (Gurdjieff, *Beelzebub's Tales to His Grandson*)	1183
Flushing the toilet	
Holiday reminders, for example, Christmas, Halloween, Thanksgiving	
Hourly "stop" on the hour	
Listening with self-consciousness	
Meals	
Mezuzah exercise: a stop in the doorway	
Opposite hand, doing things with	
Photographs, taking of oneself (Ouspensky, *In Search of the Miraculous*)	146
Praying with self-consciousness	
Sunrise (or other astronomical event) (Gurdjieff, *Beelzebub's Tales to His Grandson*)	78
Telephone	

e. The game of stops

A useful exercise that a group can use from time to time is called "The Game of Stops." It is an exercise that provides a list of suggested stops that a person can make each day for a period of several days, keeping track of how often he or she actually remembered and made the stops, as shown in Table 3 below.

List of Stops	Mo	Tu	We	Th	Fr	Sa	Su	Totals
Out of bed								
First flush								
Breakfast								
Out the door								
10:00 a.m.								
Lunch								
3:00 p.m.								
In the door								
Dinner								
Into bed								
Totals								

Table 3: The game of stops

Score yourself _____ (a perfect score is 70)

Instructions for the game of stops

1. Make each suggested stop and count up to 10 to yourself while sensing your body and dividing (expanding) your attention.

2. Continue sensing and self-remembering even after the 10 seconds for as long as possible.

3. If you miss the stop, when you do remember (before or after) also use this as an opportunity to be self-conscious and count up to 10 while body sensing.

4. At the end of each day, after the final stop, enter an X for each of your successful stops and record the total.

5. This game can be used on a weekly basis to help you to be conscious of yourself, but weeks should be skipped so that the game does not become mechanical. For the same reason, the actual stops should be varied from week to week. For example, instead of a stop at the first flush of the toilet in the morning, it could be made when the teeth are brushed. Another variation would be to engage in any activities with the hand opposite of that to which we are accustomed. Many variations are possible.

117

f. Examples of psychological exercises in alphabetical order

Individuals and groups studying *Beelzebub's Tales to His Grandson* will find suggestions for psychological Fourth Way exercises subtly given throughout the text. The following keyword list, in alphabetical order, suggests such exercises. References to page numbers in the text referring to a particular psychological state are given. Although most are from *Beelzebub's Tales to His Grandson*, a few are from related texts (as specified). Not all keywords can be related to a specific text. The list is not meant to be comprehensive and is only suggestive. It has resulted from exercises constructed by students in earlier groups based upon their insights. Students are, therefore, encouraged to construct exercises based upon their own insights that result from each new reading of the text. Consequently, the development of this list is ongoing. As always, all exercises require the dividing of attention using bodily sensation.

Keywords	Page
Adornment of one's exterior	227
Aloofness (*see* internal considering)	
Ambition	379
Anger	1205–1207
Anxiety (*see* fear)	
Arrogance	356
Avarice (*see* greed)	
Boastfulness (*see* pride, vanity)	
Bootlicking	539
Bragging	356
Buffers, identification with (Ouspensky, *In Search of the Miraculous*)	154–155
Comfort	953–957
Compassion	188
Condescension	539
Conscious labor	179, 792
Contempt	379, 384, 1194
Credulity	107
Cringing	539
Criticizing	503, 719
Cunning	379, 384, 1084
Desires, the struggle against	373
Despair	1221
Disdainfulness	28
Disease of "tomorrow"	362–364
Double-facedness	379
Doubt	736
Downing another	719

      Every kind of depravity, conscious as well as unconscious

      Feeling of self-satisfaction from leading others astray

g. Examples of exercises in page number order from *Beelzebub's Tales to His Grandson*

Individuals and groups studying *Beelzebub's Tales to His Grandson* will also find suggestions for Fourth Way exercises given throughout the text, as they read through the text page by page. The following list, in page number order, suggests exercises that may be constructed, as suggested by wording in the text. This list is not meant to be comprehensive and is only suggestive. It has resulted from exercises constructed by students in earlier groups based upon their insights. Students are, therefore, encouraged to construct exercises based upon their own insights that result from each new reading of the text. Consequently, the development of this list is ongoing. As always, all exercises require the dividing of attention using bodily sensation.

Page	Keywords
17	Obstinacy
17	Wiseacring
19–21	Identification with ownership (the Transcaucasian Kurd)
27–28	Never do as others do
28	Disdainfulness
35	If you go on a spree, go whole hog including the postage
42	Hostility
45–50	Prepare in advance for an event (the Karapet of Tiflis)
57	Irritation
71–72	Meditation (passive)
77	Remorse
78	Watching the sunrise and/or other large cosmic events
85	Unreality, seeing only
93	Do unto another's as you would do unto your own
96	Rejecting (anathematizing) another being
99	Self-love
100	Wiseacring
102	Pretense
105	Self-calming
107	Credulity, egoism, pride, self conceit, self-love, vanity
107	Suggestibility
112	Cunning
118	Identification (with the crowd or the cause)
121–129	Observation of the relativity of time
127	Hypocondria
135	Fantasizing
141	Remorse
179	Conscious labor, intentional suffering (being partkdolg-duty)

Page	Keywords
188	Compassion
188	External considering
188	Sensitivity
197	Self-calming
223	Indignaiton
223	Internal considering
223	Offended-ness
223	Pride
223	Touchiness
227	Adornment of one's exterior
242	Intentional suffering
259	Wiseacring
276	Pleasure
277	Cunning
277	Lust
295	Pride, self-love, vanity
304–305	Intuition
342–343	Morality (subjective)
356	Arrogance, bragging, imagination, pride, self-love, self-conceit
356	Swagger, vanity
362–364	Disease of tomorrow
373	Desires (the struggle against)
379	Ambition, contempt, cunning, double-facedness, envy, hate
379	Haughtiness
379	Hypocrisy, servility, slyness
384	Contempt, cunning, flattery, hate, lying, servility
387	Fear
399	Mutual inflation
405–406	Naloo-osnian impulses
423	Shame (or lack of)
426–431	Wiseacring
501	Swagger
503	Criticizing
503	Fear
539	Bootlicking, condescension, cringing, false humility
539	Haughtiness, patronization, self-abasement, sycophancy
539	Servility
554–557	Irritableness
566–567	Judgments (making of)
596	Politeness
615	Self-importance

Page	Keywords
627	Envy, jealousy, timidity
627	Hate
627	Shame (or lack of)
683	Vanity
688	Idleness
719	Criticizing, downing another, envy, jealousy, prestige
719	Wishing weakness or death in others
736	Doubt
736	Wisacring
792	Conscious labor
792	Intentional suffering
920–921	Money (identification with), preening
944–952	Food (identification with)
953–957	Comfort
954	Self-calming
960	Suggestibility
961–965	Realize the makeup of first being food
980	Self-justification
984	Laziness
1018	Infamy
1048	Envy, greed, jealousy
1074	Pride
1074	Self-love
1074	Vanity
1074–1077	Tickling
1077	Humiliation
1077	Indignation
1084	Cunning
1085	Swagger
1087	Vanity
1107	Lying
1110	Balderdash: believing in it; seeing when another puts it to you
1111	Lying
1114	Envy, jealousy
1115–1118	Cognizing imminent death
1120	Labor consciously
1131	Conscious labors and intentional sufferings
1141	External good and evil
1141	Morality (subjective)
1144	Self-calming
1160	External considering

Page	Keywords
1164	External considering
1190–1192	"I", the saying of
1194	Contempt
1194	Flattery
1194	Servility
1194	Superiority
1205–1207	Anger, internal considering
1221	Despair

Appendix 4

The plot of *Beelzebub's Tales to His Grandson*

a. Burying the dog deeper

Gurdjieff made *Beelzebub's Tales to His Grandson* intentionally difficult to approach by using cumbersome sentences and difficult language. He wrote and revised it over many years and had chapters read aloud to various groups of his students. If the deeper meanings of what he wished to convey were too clear, he would rewrite the chapter making it even more difficult to understand, because he believed that people do not value that which they acquire without effort. In explaining his frequent rewriting of the chapters in *Beelzebub's Tales to His Grandson*, Gurdjieff commented that he would have to "bury the dog deeper." [73] Some students have connected this to a common Russian expression that uses the word "dog" instead of "bone," and others to the star Sirius, known from ancient times as the "dog star." Because of difficulties that the reader may encounter, the following plot description with speculative dating is offered as an aid.

Beelzebub's Tales to His Grandson is a vast allegory set within a description of visits to and observations of the planet earth over many thousands of years, as recounted by Beelzebub who is an old and wise space traveler. In the story, Beelzebub, whom some students see as Gurdjieff himself, exploring the universe perhaps for his last time in the spaceship *Karnak*, is accompanied by his near attendants and his kinsmen, including his beloved young grandson, Hassein. He is embarked on a long space journey to attend a conference.

Many students take Hassein to represent us who sit at Gurdjieff's feet and attempt to imbibe his wisdom. During the lengthy periods of this cosmic journey there is much time for conversation, and Hassein, who has become especially interested in the strange three-brained beings (human beings) inhabiting planet earth, continually questions his grandfather about them.

It happened that previously, because of his youthful indiscretions, Beelzebub had been exiled for a very long time from the center of the universe to our remote solar system, where he took up residence on the planet Mars. From there he made six sojourns (descents) to earth covering various epochs, the first beginning during the

125

days of Atlantis and the last ending in the early 20th century. In between these visits Beelzebub continually monitored activities on earth from his base on Mars with the aid of a telescope.

To answer Hassein's many questions, Beelzebub recounts his experiences during these six visits along with the results of his telescopic observations. Through these accounts Gurdjieff's allegorical Beelzebub reveals Gurdjieff's teaching.

Because Gurdjieff made *Beelzebub's Tales to His Grandson* so difficult to approach, the new reader may give up the effort. This is especially so because the first chapter is unrelated to the story line of a space odyssey. In addition, Gurdjieff has created and used throughout the text more than 500 special words made up from a variety of languages and to which he has imparted special meanings that in many instances will not be apparent to the reader from the construction of the word.

In 1971, a Gurdjieff study group in Toronto, Canada, published a guide to these special words entitled *Guide and Index to G.I. Gurdjieff's All and Everything: Beelzebub's Tales to His Grandson*. A second edition was published in 2003. This guide takes an unusual but very useful approach in helping readers to understand *Beelzebub's Tales to His Grandson*. Over 500 special words are listed alphabetically, but rather than attempting to define each word, a task for which no one other than Gurdjieff himself was felt to be qualified, this guide shows how each word is used in various parts of the book by repeating the sentences and phrases containing the special word. From reading these sentences and phrases in the guide, the student usually can glean the meaning that Gurdjieff has intended for the special word.

The first chapter of *Beelzebub's Tales to His Grandson* is called "The Arousing of Thought." It is not part of the story, but it contains important teaching. The casual reader who chances across the book and begins to read the first few pages of text can be easily misled as to what the book is all about because the actual story line begins with chapter two. So, do not be discouraged when you read through chapter one and do not understand what the book is about. Stay with it, as the story begins with chapter two.

Most people find it easier to approach *Beelzebub's Tales to His Grandson* by reading it with others and together discussing the various themes that are presented. As we commence reading it, we should remember that the primary title of the book is *An Objectively Impartial Criticism of the Life of Man*, and that *Beelzebub's Tales to His Grandson* was initially the subtitle. The two have since been reversed. Both are included in the overall title that Gurdjieff gave to his writings, *All and Everything*, and he called this book the First Series of the three series of his writings.

b. The perturbations

In response to Hassein's questions, Beelzebub relates that during the long history of earth there have been five transapalnian perturbations or cataclysms to the planet:

1. When two parts were split off from earth by a collision with the comet Kondoor. These parts are the moon and Anulios. Anulios, like the moon, is a satellite of earth, but we cannot see Anulios because we cannot see reality.

2. The sinking of Atlantis, circa 10,000-15,000 B.C. (?)

3. Due to great winds, parts of earth were covered with sands, circa 2500 B.C. (?)

4. The great flood, circa 5500-1600 B.C. (?)

5. Possibly more covering of parts of the earth by sands, circa (?)

c. The descents

During his long banishment from the center of the universe, when he resided on Mars, Beelzebub observed the happenings on planet earth through a teskooano (telescope) that he had set up on Mars with the help of his Saturnian scientist friend, the bird-being Gornahoor Harharkh. During this period Beelzebub also made six descents [74] to earth to observe certain matters at first hand. Beelzebub relates his on-the-spot observations and his telescopic observations in response to Hassein's questions. The speculative dating and reasons for these six personal descents were:

1. During the days of Atlantis, circa 10,000-15,000 B.C. (?), to resolve difficulties caused by a member of Beelzebub's tribe. (Atlantis, if it ever existed historically, is thought to have existed from about 10,000 to 15,000 B.C., based upon Plato's comments. This dating is entirely speculative.)

2. Some 11 centuries after the first descent, to help uproot the custom of animal sacrifice (page 177 of *Beelzebub's Tales to His Grandson*).

3. A short while after the second descent, to continue to uproot the custom of animal sacrifice (page 207).

    "The coating of the said Sacred Individual [Saint Buddha] with a planetary body of a terrestrial three-brained being was actualized there several centuries before my first visit to the country Pearl-land" (India) (page 234). Historically, the Buddha is thought to have lived from 563 to 483 B.C. If this was several centuries before Beelzebub's first visit to the country of India, this first visit that is part Beelzebub's third descent would have been about 200 B.C. This is at odds with the statement that the third visit was a short while after the second descent. The second descent is stated to have been some 11 centuries after the first descent. These assertions in the text conflict with each other. Given the dating estimates for the fourth and fifth descents, it appears that the third descent was much earlier than the second or third centuries B.C.

4. After a period of rest, Beelzebub ascended to Saturn to invite Gornahoor Harharkh to descend with him back to Mars to help him arrange his telescopic observatory. While observing earth from Mars, Beelzebub and Gornahoor Harharkh became interested in the "ape question." They saw that this was agitating the three-brained beings of earth. Thus Beelzebub descended again to earth to bring back some apes to Saturn in order to carry out certain elucidating experiments. This was during the time of the beginning of Thebes, later the capital of the future Egypt, circa 3000 B.C. (?)

5. After the period of the great winds, circa 2500 B.C. (?), Beelzebub flew to earth again to elucidate the question of why the three-brained beings of earth have the periodic-need-to-destroy-the-existence-of-others-like-oneself. This is related to the question of why the lives of the three-brained beings of earth had become significantly shortened. Beelzebub had noticed these things through his telescopic observations. This was at the height of Babylonian civilization, circa 1700 B.C. (?)

6. Having noticed an increase in the process of reciprocal destruction due to the use of explosives, Beelzebub flew again to earth to better understand the strange psyche of the three-brained beings. Beelzebub tells us that this sixth descent to earth was for a period of more than 300 years, but the textual description sets most of it during the last part of the nineteenth century and the first part of the twentieth century, roughly paralleling the years of Gurdjieff's incarnation on earth.

As chapter two commences, Beelzebub had just returned to his home planet Karatas, from his sixth visit to earth. He had finally received a pardon for his youthful transgressions and was beginning his long journey to a conference being held at a planet of the pole star.

Chapters 2 through 47 are the chapters of the space odyssey.

The final chapter of *Beelzebub's Tales to His Grandson*, like the first chapter, is not part of the space odyssey, but like the first chapter, it contains important teaching. The reader who has made his or her way through the first 47 chapters of the book will certainly want to read chapter 48.

Notes

Lesson 1

1. Biblical references throughout the text are to *The Bible: New International Version*.
2. Ouspensky, *The Psychology of Man's Possible Evolution*, p. xiii.
3. Sri Madhava Ashish, in Ginsburg, *In Search of the Unitive Vision*, pp. 165–166.
4. Gurdjieff, *Life is real only then, when "I am,"* p. 23.
5. Gurdjieff, *Beelzebub's Tales to His Grandson*, p. 775.
6. In *Beelzebub's Tales to His Grandson*, Beelzebub explains that due to a cosmic calamity, even perfected beings now remain separated from the Sun-Absolute, the place where Endlessness dwells, and must remain on the planet Purgatory (the state of perfected being) but impossible of complete unity with Endlessness so long as the universe remains in manifestation. Theologians are divided as to whether it is possible for there to be a complete return to the source.
7. See Ouspensky, *In Search of the Miraculous*, p. 44.
8. Gurdjieff, *Views from the Real World*, p. 58.

Lesson 2

9. Gurdjieff, *Views from the Real World*, p. 148.
10. Ouspensky, *In Search of the Miraculous*, p. 119.
11. Sri Madhava Ashish, in Ginsburg, *In Search of the Unitive Vision*, p. 224.

Lesson 3

12. Gurdjieff, *Beelzebub's Tales to His Grandson*, p. 386.
13. For an English translation of the Vedic references, see Pannikkar, *The Vedic Experience, Mantramanjari*, pp. 557, 560, 598, 715, 741.
14. Ouspensky, *In Search of the Miraculous*, p. 294.
15. Modified from Nicoll, *Psychological Commentaries on the Teachings of G.I. Gurdjieff and P.D. Ouspensky*, vol. II, p. 388.

Lesson 4

16. Ouspensky, *In Search of the Miraculous*, pp. 150–151.
17. Gurdjieff, *Beelzebub's Tales to His Grandson*, p. 1164.

Lesson 5

18. Gurdjieff, *Views from the Real World*, p. 78.
19. Gurdjieff, *Beelzebub's Tales to His Grandson*, p. 355.
20. Sri Madhava Ashish, in Ginsburg, *In Search of the Unitive Vision*, pp. 165–166.
21. Blavatsky, *The Voice of the Silence*, p. 17.

22. Blavatsky, *The Secret Doctrine*, vol. II, p. 20.

23. See Gurdjieff's views on our mistaken idea that we need lots of sleep in *Views from the Real World*, p. 119.

24. Merton, *New Seeds of Contemplation*, pp. 226–228.

25. Sri Madhava Ashish, in Ginsburg, *In Search of the Unitive Vision*, p. 226.

26. Sri Madhava Ashish, in Ginsburg, *In Search of the Unitive Vision*, p. 226.

Lesson 6

27. Gurdjieff, *Beelzebub's Tales to His Grandson*, p. v.

28. De Dampierre, interviewed by Le Vallois, "Sacred Dance: The Search for Conscious Harmony."

29. Moore, *Gurdjieff: The Anatomy of a Myth*, pp. 353–355.

30. Merton, *New Seeds of Contemplation*, p. 228.

31. Sri Madhava Ashish, in Ginsburg, *In Search of the Unitive Vision*, p. 281.

Appendix 1

32. Excerpted and modified from Ginsburg, "Gurdjieff, Blavatsky and the Masters of Wisdom," pp. 43–73.

33. Zber, *Who are you Monsieur Gurdjieff?* p. 10.

34. Zber, *Who are you Monsieur Gurdjieff?* p. 65.

35. Gurdjieff, *Beelzebub's Tales to His Grandson*, p. 347.

36. Ginsburg, *In Search of the Unitive Vision*, p. 138.

37. Blavatsky's works have been collected and published in 14 volumes by the Theosophical Publishing House, under the title *The Collected Writings of H.P. Blavatsky*.

38. Blavatsky, *The Secret Doctrine*, vol. II, pp. 797–798.

39. Blavatsky, *The Secret Doctrine*, vol. II, p. 437.

40. Blavatsky, *The Secret Doctrine*, vol. I, p. xl.

41. Blavatsky, *The Secret Doctrine*, vol. I, p. xxxviii.

42. Ouspensky, *In Search of the Miraculous*, p. 64.

43. Blavatsky, *The Secret Doctrine*, vol. II, p. 437.

44. Blavatsky, *The Secret Doctrine*, vol. II, p. 437.

45. Details of the possible connection between Gurdjieff, Gurdjieff's students, and the publication of the Mahatma Letters were reported by Moore in "The Blavatsky–Gurdjieff question: a footnote on Maude Hoffman and A.T. Barker," p. 77.

46. Walker, *A Study of Gurdjieff's Teaching*, p. 152. No record of this letter, nor to whom it was sent, is given by Walker.

47. Gurdjieff, *Beelzebub's Tales to His Grandson*, p. 50.

Appendix 2

48. Gurdjieff, *Views from the Real World*, 115–123.

49. Gurdjieff, *Views from the Real World*, p. 117.

50. See Anderson, *The Fiery Fountains*.

51. See Jung, *Man and His Symbols*.

52. Nicoll, *Psychological Commentaries on the Teaching of G.I. Gurdjieff and P.D. Ouspensky*, vol. I, 353–354.

53. Anderson, *The Unknowable Gurdjieff*, p. 54.

54. Gurdjieff, *Beelzebub's Tales to His Grandson*, pp. 359–360.

55. Ouspensky, *In Search of the Miraculous*, p. 194.

56. Ouspensky, *In Search of the Miraculous*, p. 150.

57. Gurdjieff, *Beelzebub's Tales to His Grandson*, pp. 372–373.

58. Gurdjieff, *Views from the Real World*, p. 50.

59. See Ginsburg, "Gurdjieff and the teaching on dreams."

60. Sri Madhava Ashish, in Ginsburg, *In Search of the Unitive Vision*, p. 15.

61. Gurdjieff, *Beelzebub's Tales to His Grandson*, p. 1164.

62. Gurdjieff, *Beelzebub's Tales to His Grandson*, p. 792.

63. Sri Madhava Ashish, in Ginsburg, *In Search of the Unitive Vision*, p. 137.

64. Sri Madhava Ashish, in Ginsburg, *In Search of the Unitive Vision*, p. 233.

65. Sri Madhava Ashish, in Ginsburg, *In Search of the Unitive Vision*, pp. 275.

66. Sri Madhava Ashish, in Ginsburg, *In Search of the Unitive Vision*, pp. 120–124.

67. Ginsburg, *In Search of the Unitive Vision*, p. 40–41.

68. "Noumenal" is used here to mean "real" in the Gurdjieffian sense of "the real world."

69. Sri Madhava Ashish, in Ginsburg, *In Search of the Unitive Vision*, pp. 41–42.

70. Gurdjieff, *Views from the Real World*, p. 119.

Appendix 3

71. Sri Madhava Ashish, in Ginsburg, *In Search of the Unitive Vision*, p. 224.

72. Merton, *New Seeds of Contemplation*, p. 226.

Appendix 4

73. Bennett, *Gurdjieff: Making a New World*, p. 274.

74. Some students of hermeticism have attributed an altogether different allegorical meaning to the six "descents." In this alternative view, the descents are seen as meditative descents into the mind. See Lonsdale, *Gurdjieff and the Arch Preposterous*, p. 17.

Works cited

Anderson, M. *The Fiery Fountains*. New York: Hermitage House, 1951.

Anderson, M. *The Unknowable Gurdjieff*. New York: Samuel Weiser, 1972.

Bennett, J. G. *Gurdjieff: Making a New World*. New York: Harper & Row, 1973.

Blavatsky, H.P. *The Collected Writings of H.P. Blavatsky*, compiled by B. de Zirkoff, 14 vols. Wheaton: Theosophical Publishing House, 1966–1985.

Blavatsky, H.P. *The Secret Doctrine: The Synthesis of Science, Religion and Philosophy*, 2 vols. London: Theosophical Publishing House, 1888. Los Angeles: The Theosophy Company, facsimile reprint, 1974.

Blavatsky, H.P. *The Voice of the Silence*, 1889. Wheaton: Quest–Theosophical Publishing House, facsimile reprint, 1991.

De Dampierre, P., interviewed by J. Le Vallois. "Sacred Dance: The Search for Conscious Harmony." *The American Theosophist*, 1985, Spring Special Issue, pp. 175–181.

Ginsburg, S.B. *In Search of the Unitive Vision: Letters of Sri Madhava Ashish to an American Businessman, 1978–1997*. Boca Raton: New Paradigm Books, 2001.

Ginsburg, S.B. "Gurdjieff and the Teaching on Dreams." *Stopinder*, No. 7, Winter 2002.

Ginsburg, S.B. "Gurdjieff, Blavatsky and the Masters of Wisdom." In *Proceedings of the Third International Humanities Conference: All and Everything '98*, edited by H.J. Sharp. Bognor Regis, private printing, 1998.

Gurdjieff, G.I. *All and Everything: Ten Books in Three Series. First Series: An Objectively Impartial Criticism of the Life of Man or Beelzebub's Tales to His Grandson*. New York: Harcourt Brace and Company, 1950; Penguin/Arkana, 1999.

Gurdjieff, G.I. *Second Series: Meetings with Remarkable Men*, translated by A.R. Orage. New York: E.P. Dutton, 1963.

Gurdjieff, G.I. *Third Series: Life is real only then, when "I am,"* New York: Triangle Editions, 1975.

Gurdjieff, G.I. *Views from the Real World: Early talks of Gurdjieff*. New York: Triangle Editions, 1973; Penguin/Arkana, 1984.

Gurdjieff study group. *Guide and Index to G.I. Gurdjieff's Beelzebub's Tales to His Grandson*, 2nd edn. Toronto: Traditional Studies Press, 2003.

Jung, C.G. *Man and His Symbols*. London: Aldus Books, 1964.

Lonsdale, J. *Gurdjieff and the Arch-Preposterous*. Sydney: Image DTP, 2000.

Merton, T. *New Seeds of Contemplation*. New York: Penguin New Directions, 1962.

Moore, J. *Gurdjieff: The Anatomy of a Myth*. Shaftesbury, Dorset, and Rockport, MA: Element, 1991.

Moore J. "The Blavatsky–Gurdjieff question: a footnote on Maude Hoffman and A.T. Barker." *Theosophical History*, 1990, vol. 3, no. 3.

Nicoll, M. *Psychological Commentaries on the Teaching of G.I. Gurdjieff and P.D. Ouspensky*, 5 vols. London: Robinson & Watkins, 1952.

Ouspensky, P.D. *In Search of the Miraculous*. London: Routledge & Kegan Paul, 1950; Harvest/HBJ, 1974.

Ouspensky, P.D. *The Psychology of Man's Possible Evolution*. New York: Knopf, 1954; Vintage Books, 1974.

Ouspensky, P.D. *Tertium Organum: The Third Canon of Thought, a Key to the Enigmas of the World*, translated by N. Bessaroff and C. Bragdon. New York: Knopf, 1945.

Pannikkar, R. *The Vedic Experience, Mantramanjari*. Delhi: Motilal Banarsidass Publishers, 1983, 2001.

Walker, K. *A Study of Gurdjieff's Teaching*. London: Jonathan Cape, 1957.

Zuber, R. *Who Are You Monsieur Gurdjieff?* London: Routledge & Kegan Paul, 1980.

Index

ABOUT THE AUTHOR

Seymour B. (Sy) Ginsburg was born in Chicago, Illinois, in 1934, and graduated from Northwestern University with degrees in accountancy and law. He was a founder of a predecessor business and the first president of Toys R Us, and afterward a member of the Chicago Mercantile Exchange. On a private visit to India in 1978, he met the guru, Sri Madhava Ashish, who advised him: "If you want to study in a Western way the path that we follow here at Mirtola, you need to study and work with the Gurdjieff teaching." Sy is active in the Theosophical Society and was president of the Theosophical Society in South Florida for many years. He was a founder of the Gurdjieff Institute of Florida, and has been a student of Theosophy and of Gurdjieff's teaching for more than 25 years. With his wife Dorothy, he currently divides his time between South Florida and Chicago, where he periodically gives this introductory course on Gurdjieff's teaching to introduce the teaching to those who may be interested.

In Search of the Unitive Vision: Letters of Sri Madhava Ashish to an American Businessman, 1978–1997, compiled with a commentary by Seymour B. Ginsburg, (New Paradigm, 2001) gives an account of the teaching he received from the British–Indian guru living in the Himalayas who offered Sy the solution to his own personal difficulties and to the larger problems of our troubled world by the discovery of what he calls, the "unitive vision."